Searching Out Loud: Giving Voice to Independent Investigations

Searching Out Loud

Giving Voice to Independent Investigations

A Digital Media and Information Literacy Curriculum for
Reporters, Researchers, and Legal Professionals

UNIT FIVE:

*HOW TO PRESENT WHAT WE LEARN IN
TEACHABLE WAYS AND TO USEFUL OUTCOMES*

ISBN (978-1-7332554-8-6) print version
ISBN (978-1-7332554-6-2) e-book version

Some characters and events in this book are fictitious. Any similarity to real persons, living or dead, is coincidental and not intended by the author.

Promotion of the books, tools, applications, and creative works of...
 Romantic Deception by Dr. Sally Caldwell and Darlene E. Adams
 Finding Birthdays and Related Persons in One Step by Stephen P. Morse
 SurfWax search engine by Tom Holt
 Gigablast search engine by Matt Wells
 L-Soft and LISTSERV® trademark by L-Soft International, Inc.
 SearchEngineLand by ThirdDoorMedia.com
 WorldCat image and trademark by OCLC.org
 BRB Public Records by BRB Publications, LLC

Reprinted by permission.

Book Design by Davin Pasek and Emma Koramshahi of Paradise Copies
All photographs by the author unless otherwise credited.

Printed and bound in USA
First Printing September 2019

Published by The Society of Useful Information
4 French Street
Hadley, MA 01035

Visit www.searchingoutloud.org

For Patty, who taught me the root of all source knowledge:
Enduring gratitude

"I was gratified to be able to answer promptly, and I did. I said I didn't know."

— **Mark Twain**

"The most courageous act is still to think for yourself. Aloud."

— **Coco Chanel**

"No provider or user of an interactive computer service shall be treated as the publisher or speaker of any information provided by another information content provider."

— **Communications Decency Act, Section 230**

SEARCHING OUT LOUD
GIVING VOICE TO INDEPENDENT INVESTIGATIONS

CURRICULUM GUIDE

Here is the structure used for organizing the book along with the chapters for delivering the methods and skills for becoming Knowledge-ABLED through the Searching Out Loud digital literacy curriculum.

===

UNIT ONE:
How to Turn Information into Knowledge
Preparing:
How to Project Manage Virtual Investigations

===

UNIT ONE SUMMARY

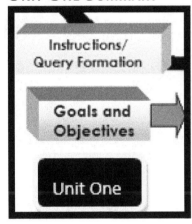

Our first section addresses search project management ("SPM"). SPM is based on the simple and often overlooked reality that being online costs a great deal; not in connect charges or even subscription fees but just by the shear amount of time we invest in searching, often with little to show for it.

Regardless of leaps in processing power, portability, and media convergence, there will remain a single problem reducible to two perennial questions: (1) what kinds of information are out there; and (2) how can what I'm looking for explain or even shape the decisions and actions I'll be making or revising?

SPM contains the discipline and focus that transcends technological change. In **Unit One** we apply SPM principles to recurring research assignments by setting out our information goals. To do this, we'll begin by defining what separates high from low quality information in pursuit of our project objectives. Then we'll decide on the appropriate research approach to our mission-specific projects. Finally, SPM gives us the focus to manage our search projects effectively so that the time and effort we invest is in line with the results we get online.

UNIT ONE SECTION STRUCTURE

1.1 Search Project Management: How do we assess what we want from our research sessions before we log into them

> a. How information becomes useful knowledge in pursuit of project goals and search targets

> b. An overview of the digital discovery process from initial exploration to knowledge mapping and informed decision-making

1.2 Search Logs: How do we document the successes and failures of our research according to the goals and objectives of our investigations

> ■ Pursuing search targets with discipline through selective documentation and action-based questions

1.3 Blindspots: What are some common traps and limitations that impede independent investigations and our effectiveness as researchers

> ■ Setting our information radar to gauge the awareness levels and blindspots of our search targets

1.4 Becoming Knowledge-ABLED: What is our role in bridging the divide between the communities we serve and the technologies that serve us as researchers

> a. What do search engines do and how do they work

> b. How search engines process information, where they get their processing, and how we can get them to do our bidding

Unit One Benefits

> ■ Learn and adopt SPM – A step-by-step process that helps us take control of Internet searches

> ■ Set goals, milestones, and resource limits for finding and applying pertinent information to our research projects

> ■ Build information radars that reveal where our search targets are spending their time and attention and where they're distracted or unaware (blindspots)

> ■ Identify the culprits that steal time from our virtual investigations so we can bypass them when they next arise

> ■ Figure in the time and expense we save by applying sound site selection practices

> ■ Calculate the value accrued in billing for our research services

Unit One Tables

> ■ The Knowledge Continuum – The challenge of using the web for research

> ■ Search Project Management steps and examples - Putting our cards on the table through search logs

> ■ Example search logs – Travel agents, caregivers, criminal investigators

> ■ Google search trade-offs for researchers - Working within search engine limitations

===

UNIT TWO:
How to Search for Information That Informs
Seeking:
Using Search in Virtual Investigations

===

Unit Two Summary

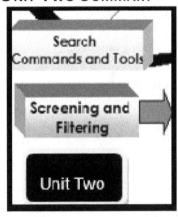

Unit Two is about tossing out the Driver's Ed instruction manual, getting in the car, and taking our established interests and new skills out for a test drive. **Unit Two** applies what we've learned about how search works to different engine and directory options. The goal is to conduct sophisticated, time-effective searches with a minimum of preparation and fees. Our priority is to focus on the best available tool and search strategy for the job at hand.

Having looked under the search engine hood in **Unit One**, we'll focus on tool selection, query formation, and refinement. We'll differentiate and select the right digital search and discovery tools, including visualization, cluster and NLP engines, as well as automated and human-filtered subject directories.

Next we start our meaningful exchanges with these tools by building effective queries. This means using the right search commands and word selection options for leveraging Internet resources, using correct syntax and semantics to express ourselves, and applying fact- and opinion-based guidelines to create productive outcomes.

Finally we draw on search operators, unique IDs, and pointers to either generalize or specify around the topics or our search targets – those events, policies, procedures, groups, or people in question. Our choices will depend not only on how but where we set our sights in the form of site selection.

UNIT TWO SECTION STRUCTURE

2.1 Query Formation: How to arrange, express, generalize, and specify our research questions

    a. What's a fair question and how to interview a search engine

    b. Conveying our intentions through syntax and search operators

    c. Refinements and corrections through term expansion and contraction

2.2 Semantics: What are the best terms for conducting research

    a. The role of informed word choice for building intentionality into search statements

    b. Applying unique IDs and verbatims to exact match and people searches

2.3 Tool Selection: What research tool to use and for which job

    a. Determining the right digital search and discovery tools for the questions we're raising, including visualization, cluster, metasearch and NLP engines

    b. Deciding on the right reference tools and recognized authorities in the fields we're searching including social media, portals, and subject directories

    c. Working with search engines, subject directories, or specialty databases when it's generalities, specifics, or somewhere in-between

2.4 Site Selection: Searching beyond search engines

    a. Where to do research and why size and location matters

    b. Determining the best starting point for the task at-hand

    c. Adjusting our approach to fit our resources

Unit Two Benefits

- Pose productive questions with a bias towards action

- Recognize appropriate search commands and word selection options for leveraging Internet resources

- Arrange and express effective search queries by using correct syntax and semantics

- Yield productive outcomes by applying fact- and opinion-based searches

- Generalize or specify around our topics and search targets by drawing on search operators, unique IDs, and pointers

- Overcome common pitfalls including familiar search detours, poor indexing, and character limits

- Reshape a misinformed question by redirecting our focus to more common problem sets and suggested searches

Unit Two Tables

- Defining what matters – The secret sauce of ordering search results through keywords, repetition, verbatims, and proximity

- Overcoming search limits – What we need to teach the search engine that it can't possibly know

- The haystacks and icebergs framework – Learning cues for opinion and fact-based searches

- Dialogging with search results through SEO (search engine optimization), unique IDs and pointers

- Answers, not documents – Defining natural language search engines

- Overlay of engines and directories – Precision versus recall

===

UNIT THREE:
How to Source Information That Instructs
Sourcing:
How to Evaluate Information Quality

===

UNIT THREE SUMMARY

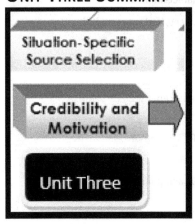

Unit Three focuses on acquiring source fluency and learning how to leverage those sources to improve the quality of the information you source virtually. The Unit starts by confronting the essential form of how information is delivered to us and the questions it inspires: Where is it located? What is it called? When was it done? Who did it? Why do I care? How do I find it again?

We can't possibly know everything and this is no less true for sourcing the world's knowledge. Committing an inventory of leading references and go-to experts on any subject is too daunting even for the reference librarians. Our goal is not to become librarians but to develop a skill called source fluency. Source fluency ensures that we're looking in the right place – even when we're a first-time visitor to unfamiliar topics. We'll set up a quality control process that not only reduces the search noise that clutters our screens. It also helps us to attract, analyze, and interpret the sources we need to fulfill our project objectives. We'll develop the quality of our findings on three levels: Search sets, websites, and individual pages (but only the ones worth opening)!

Unit Three is also devoted to unlocking the secrets, pitfalls and potentials of searching topic-focused Internet databases. Building on our **Unit Two** understanding of search engines (oceans) and subject directories (lakes), we'll dive into the information pond of more narrow and targeted specialty databases to uncover scarce and often overlooked information. OLP ("Oceans, Lakes, and Ponds") is the primary method for establishing: (1) source fluency, and (2) for determining *when* to pursue *what size* database in our virtual investigations.

UNIT THREE SECTION STRUCTURE

3.1 Information Types: How to integrate search findings into a useful form

    a. Surviving the search results page

    b. How information gets packaged in four dimensions – Entry-based, resource-based, view-based, and form-based

3.2 Source Fluency: How to cast our search nets for building source credibility and confidence

    a. Applying the concept of OLP ("Oceans, Lakes, and Ponds") to source the web

    b. Developing source fluency so we can apply sound sourcing methods no matter who's supplying the content

    c. How far to push and how deep to dig before drawing conclusions or reaching out to others

3.3 Quality Control: How to evaluate Information

    a. The three levels of quality control for skimming and assessing results sets, websites, and individual pages

    b. Determining when to use what source, including premium (fee-based) information and deep web (a.k.a. 'invisible web') sources

3.4 Managing Project Resources: How to price information's time and money dimensions

    a. Sizing up free versus fee – When it makes sense to use premium content and where to find it for minimal cost

    b. Using content groupings and specialty collections to narrow in on specifics or expand on topics

Unit Three Benefits

- Use appropriate techniques to analyze, interpret, and attract the sources you need to fulfill search objectives

- Regulate information quality – Focusing exclusively on sources worthy of our review

- Conduct an editorial check to qualify web-based publications

- Formulas to qualify resources, quantify our confidence in them, and avert the need to open individual pages

- Recognize where the likely boundary lies between public and proprietary information

- Know and apply the rules for uncovering overlooked information

- Reap the benefits of grouping sources for justifying our source choices

- Determine when the media becomes the story and not just the source of it

Unit Three Tables

- Quantity controls for testing the waters – Ratio of key indicators including the Google sniff test, and signal-to-noise formulas

- Link analysis for understanding the scope and reach of information providers

- The deep versus the shallow web – Why two Internets

- The media dietary chain – Recognizing source self-interest

- Using premium databases for climbing out of an information ditch

===

UNIT FOUR:
Sense-making:
Focusing on Information Context

===

UNIT FOUR SUMMARY

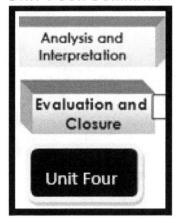

Unit Four has two principle thrusts: (1) Approaching research social networks as a researcher; and (2), engaging them as a member, including how to screen, join, attract, and communicate through virtual communities.

The slippery distinction between observer and participant is especially sensitive as we shift from the 'searching' to 'conversing'' phase of our research projects. This section focuses on ways to trail and gather background details on search targets that generate digital identities through their social media profiles, networks, and commentary.

The model we use for reading networks and acting on them is called provider conjugation. Like verb conjugation, this tool helps to establish the flow and context of how information travels and the perceptions it carries with it. We also apply it to ourselves as information providers in determining the perceptions we want to form about us. This includes the types of contacts we want to attract and build into our own networks – especially in reaching out to search targets that prove to be social media party animals, digital hermits, or somewhere in-between.

UNIT FOUR SECTION STRUCTURE

4.1. Provider Conjugation: How to determine the motives of information providers in groups and as individuals

> a. Defining senders, recipients and audiences to understand the direction and speed that information travels

> b. Assessing the nature and trade-offs of individuals and groups as information sources

> c. Leveraging lateral thinking as a tool for conducting Internet research

4.2 Misinformation as an information source: How to use information rather than *be used* by it

> a. Taking the sniff test to grounded or unfounded suspicions

> b. Decoding the role that gatekeepers, watchdogs, and regulators play in scandal-making

> c. Picking up the scent of smoking guns – Red flag conditions for conflicts of interest

> d. Opinions online – How to know who is gaming the system or fabricating their credentials

4.3 The value of social information: Applying provider conjugation to social media

> a. Using social bookmarking to vet source experts

> b. Trapping information through RSS feeds to target new opportunities

> c. Building custom search applications to uncover key details

> d. Gaining media cachet through blogging and selective interviewing

> e. Joining a professional network, cultivating contacts

4.4 Search to Converse: How to get from reading about others to direct engagement

> a. The giant listening ear as a networking asset

> b. Bartering information among groups and individuals

Unit Four Benefits

- Background research the people you're going to meet – Deploy specialized search tools to gauge their web presence and digital identities

- Build a stable of advisers and referral networks for finding experts and second opinions

- Assess the differences between the way information is communicated informally through word-of-mouth and institutionally through groups

- Apply the Vectors of Integrity to determine the credibility of information providers and their own involvement in the issues they report

- Gauge the reputation of our search targets (it's not in the eye of the beholder)!

- Leverage social networking tools to raise our digital profile as an independent investigator

- Use alerts and notifications to stay on top of fluid and evolving situations

- Pick a blog theme that can be strengthened by our research

Unit Four Tables

- Social Networks – From soul searching to role seeking

- Using link analysis to determine social circles

- Common tagging concepts for breaking new ground and reclaiming past breakthroughs

- The Seven Vectors of Relationship Integrity – Using online communities to weigh objective and subjective-based experience

- Credibility Pyramid – The scale of public scrutiny

- Cultivating contacts – Defining boundaries and fail-safes

===

UNIT FIVE:
How to Present What We Learn in Teachable Ways
Presenting:
How to Connect What You Learn to Useful Outcomes

===

Unit Five Summary

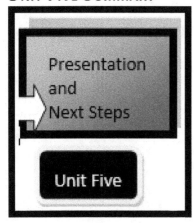

We talk about opportunities when we use information. We think in terms of risk when others do so. **Unit Five** focuses not only on what we learn but how this works in relation to what others know and perceive. How can we as messengers assess the nerves we strike and the buttons we push in the research we're delivering?

The first four units focus on how to gather information and act on it. **Unit Five** is about how others will act on the research we deliver through social media and more formal, offline channels: The reports and presentations to peers, clients, and groups (our "audience"). How will our findings be interpreted and acted on? How we deliver them is every bit as important as the research itself.

Unit Five brings together the search project management steps, query formation, quality controls, source fluency and information conjugation methods to deliver your research to the clients, colleagues, and communities we're supporting. These message receivers will clearly see how your informed use of web research tools and practices is bringing value, economy, and even closure to complex and resource-hungry investigations. We will then turn our attention to the report itself, coming to grips with the news we're delivering, the explanatory power of our analysis, and the changes we're proposing.

UNIT FIVE SECTION STRUCTURE

5.1 Message Delivery: How to Knowledge-ENABLE our colleagues, clients and community through our findings, analysis, reporting, and recommended actions

> a. Confirmable Outcomes – Reducing uncertainty, building consensus, and making reasonable assertions from complex and resource-hungry investigations

> b. Results Verification –- *Closing the loop* between the words and deeds as well as the facts and opinions documented through our search logs

5.2 Information Packaging: Bringing together the SPM structure, query formation, source fluency, and information conjugation to deliver winning reports

> a. Packaging the results – What they should contain, what to leave out, and how they should unfold as a learning narrative

> b. Assimilating search results, coverage patterns, and those elusive, missing pieces to draw meaningful comparisons and spotlight where the real story lies

5.3 Project Presentation: Conclusions, recommendations and next steps

> a. Drawing the line between independent investigators and the dependent actors we investigate

> b. Presenting clear and useful follow-up actions to clients and stakeholders without falling into decision-making traps

5.4 Post Investigation: Information-coping skills for self-managing our digital interactions

> a. Keeping the right doors open for continual discovery and professional growth

> b. Applying research disciplines to routines for managing our personal brands, virtual identities, and offline realities

Unit Five Benefits

- Differentiate deliberate from serendipitous discoveries

- Pinpoint conflicts of interest among our search targets

- Know where the bones are buried *before* you dig them up

- Legitimize the correct claims about conflicting facts and numbers

- Know and document the difference between confirmable facts and educated guesses

- Map research to primary intelligence and opportunities to barter information

- Assess the attention paid to our search topic and/or target and the broader issues they address

Unit Five Tables

■ The certainty continuum for assessing the black and white (and gray)

■ The candor of strangers and the corrupting influence of friendship

■ The compromises to sound judgment posed by instant information

■ Conversational icebreakers for breaking the case wide open

■ Discussion maps for connecting the interests of our search targets to our project goals

==

UNIT SIX:
The Knowledge-ABLED Cook Book
Using Information:
A Recipe for Success

==

UNIT SIX SUMMARY

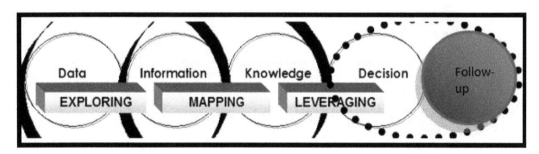

The book concludes with a Knowledge-ABLED use case based on the professional transformation of a commercial video producer to an educational media consultant. This use case guides us through the false starts and initial frustrations to the firmer footing and ultimate confidence-building that comes with being knowledge-ENABLED.

All relevant practices, frameworks, and search strategies in the case study are referenced to the specific units and chapters where they're introduced and demonstrated. For instance our use case subject entrepreneur plots out his research goals and supporting tasks through the Search Project Management model.

He applies the principles of site selection and Oceans, Lakes and Ponds to determine his sources, generate business leads, and build his understanding of the market and its growth potential. Finally he uses provider conjugation as a way of engaging the very same business contacts that first landed on his radar as search targets.

This journey is mapped out in three sections:

> **1. The Diagnosis** – We find out what makes our entrepreneur tick, how he's transitioning careers, and his challenges both as a researcher and a marketer.

> **2. The Search** – We apply the models and methods introduced in the first five units of the book to help scale the virtual research walls that were blocking the entrepreneur in the first section of **Unit Six**.

> **3. The Engagement** – We see the pay offs from the results of Part Two through our subject's ability to generate business leads, develop networking contacts, and narrow down to a selective and promising market niche.

UNIT SIX SECTION STRUCTURE

6.1 Introduction: Food for thought: you are what you eat

> a. Defining culinary metaphors and applying them to the research process, such as...

> b. Main ingredients, meal types, cuisines, courses and cooking methods

6.2 The Diagnosis: Assessing the goals and challenges of our case subject

> a. Initial intake – Coming to terms with internet confusion

> b. Better business targeting through site selection – Building credibility through reporting requirements

> c. Defining the boundaries – Scoping out the SPM to keep the project online and in line with our objectives

6.3 The Search: Matching the pursuit to the pay-offs

> a. The information ocean for generating and qualifying business leads

> b. The information lake for assessing market studies

> c. The information pond to get from trapping to acting on what we learn

> d. The book on RSS feed readers and their functions and benefits

6.4 The Engagement: The transition from searching to conversing

> a. Listening to markets – How to use RSS as a survey tool for mapping and confirming trends

> b. A review of the site selection techniques used to uncover the sources used in the case study

> c. The provider conjugation method for assessing the motives of information suppliers and how our subject is viewed by others as an information provider in his own right

Unit Six Benefits

> ■ Use term expansion to segment markets

> ■ Understand the situational specifics and efficiencies in the local search, clipping, and alerting functions of RSS readers

> ■ Connect individual experts to their key affiliations and then learn which groups are worth approaching

> ■ Generate feeds from news queries, news sites, and social media sources (event triggers)

> ■ Design a proactive follow-up to business leads triggered by daily events

Unit Six Tables

- Assembling the meal
- Gathering the research
- Mapping OLP to actions and outcomes
- Search Project Management Plan for our use case, (a.k.a. "George Reis Productions")

*While not part of the curriculum guide, **Unit Seven** lays out next steps for applying the perennial lessons of Searching Out Loud in the changing dynamics between information providers and tomorrow's Knowledge-ABLED investigators.*

INTRODUCTION:
Searching Out Loud
Giving Voice to Independent
Investigations

Searches

No one likes to search.

Everyone likes to find — especially when we find evidence that reaffirms our conclusions and validates our hunches.

That works out fine if we're trying to determine what model of which version to park in our shopping carts or determining which pizzeria prepares the tastiest toppings within proximity to our locations and price points.

Finding search results that comport to our own purchase criteria and shopping cycles might support our preferences for quality, expedience, and even personal fulfillment. However, those same calculations might prejudice or even misguide our ability process to uphold, protect, and honor the people and institutions we have agreed to serve and represent.

It is this wider notion of community purpose and civic engagement that is entrusted to the reader, not the social media platform or search engine claiming to find results for us, regardless of our searching abilities.

Search is more than a command box, virtual confession booth, or answers mediated by machines. It is the foundation for the independence of thought required to fulfill our civic duties. This book is about posing our natural curiosities to a world of preformed and often artificial responses. It is a search that we form on our own that answers to this larger socially-minded concern.

A search that comes to us is surely predisposed to the very same biases and assumptions that limit our effectiveness as citizen-users of an Internet-based investigation. The Knowledge-ABLED approach is one that combines this wider social concern in the pursuit of impartiality, empiricism, and integrity. These aims are not considered, supported, or factored into the commercial objectives of big search: Those companies who benefit directly from grabbing hold of the steering wheel that interprets, navigates, and brokers our use of the web.

The evidence-gathering of these intended search objectives purges those assumptions, biases, and conceits of near-certain conclusions. There is simply no other path to decisions reached by elevated perspectives, open minds, and the unknowable destinations of a Knowledge-ABLED investigation.

INVESTIGATIONS

In the late summer of 2018, the American popular imagination was transfixed on the momentousness of one national decision. It was the confirmation vote for Brett Kavanaugh to the U.S. Supreme Court.

Beyond Justice Kavanaugh's fate, this was a vote that would determine the direction of the one government above the fray. The branch shielded from the pressures of election campaigns and accountability of election cycles. This was the institution that remained faithful to the rule of law, a guarantee of an *independent* judiciary.

On the Senate floor there were no such principles on display or built into the backroom deliberations of its members. Neither party had the stomach, grace, or latitude to dignify the merit of the other side's concerns. Ninety-eight of one hundred votes were cast along party lines. Those breaking ranks synchronized their dissenting votes to not be the deciding ones. Not a shred of integrity was evident on the Senate floor. After all the motions, no one had budged, except in acknowledging the need to beef-up Senate security in the wake of anonymous threats from outside the chamber.

Amid the accusations, and bombast, we onlookers observed one additional basis for agreement between the opposing parties:

> This was no way to conduct a confirmation hearing.

Far from a consensus, the only sliver of movement in this intractable mess was the move for an independent investigation. A fact-finding mission by a non-political actor might break the logjam by providing a more guarded forum for witnesses to come forward, for investigators to consider the emerging patterns, and for an overheated country to step back from the intensity of such a politically charged outcome. In effect it wasn't our faith in the political process or our institutions that was going to move us from splintering factions to a binding decision. It was the findings of an outside arm of the government whose job was to steer clear of the same preformed conclusions depended on by one hundred U.S. Senators.

This was our best hope as a country to preserve an independent jury.

© CSPAN: Supreme Court Nominee Brett Kavanaugh and Senator Dianne Feinstein, Confirmation Hearing, Day 3, Part 6

WHEN SEARCHES MEET INVESTIGATIONS

Searches meet investigations and out comes the info.

Information:

> 1. It's a renewable resource.
>
> 2. It's the lifeblood of a knowledge economy.

When we determine its worth, we surmise...

> ■ There's too much of it.
>
> ■ Too little of it means very much.

This begs a followup question: What makes information less abstract and more meaningful? When we ascribe a will to it, we learn that it "wants to be free." But what do we want out of the deal? Certainly something more aspirational than free information. We want information that informs. Now the conversation turns to knowledge:

> 1. It's power.
>
> 2. It's the economic heart of our material abundance.

Measure the world in units of knowledge and...

> ■ No one suffers from an abundance of it.
>
> ■ If anything there's a scarcity of it.

What would it take to close that deficit?

What's the most popular one-word definition of knowledge? It's power. And we appreciate that before we even know what to do with our knowledge.

But here's the rub.

Information wants to be free and knowledge doesn't aspire to anything. Power closes down dissent and debate. Knowledge is an open book. It's a quality that many of us covet more than any capture-worthy material or ideal we could ever hope to possess. So here's the question: How do we get from *free* to *power*? They're not polar opposites but they're not exactly complementary. Or are they?

This book is about how to take a surplus and narrow a deficit. In our case the abundance is in the volume of available information. The scarcity is an understanding of what to do with it.

The difference between collecting online information and putting it to use starts with a better understanding of how it operates – how it behaves once activated by our thirst for knowledge, and yes, our lust for power.

What's information behavior? It sounds like something we observe in a lab facility as part of an advanced degree program – too complex for mere mortals like us to grasp! Information behavior sounds like we'd need to pass through security and a web of high-ranking advisers in order to understand it, reason with it, and ultimately act on it.

What we'll do is break information down so that it is understandable to us investigators (its pursuers). No matter how advanced or plain and simple our understanding of the actual information happens to be, that means unpacking our pursuits according to:

> 1. **Substance:** The content and purpose of the information.
>
> 2. **Form:** What shape the information is created in and/or packaged and distributed.
>
> 3. **Perception:** How the content is received by the folks relevant to our investigation both in the way it's delivered and the degree of certainty it conveys through its form and substance.

That's right. Useful information boils down to form, substance, and perception – not rocket science or brain surgery. It's one thing to conclude that what we see and hear influences what we think and say. It's quite another to see how our own influence is determined by how others come to process, understand, and act on the information that finds them.

We'll get back to substance, form, and perception in a moment. But first let's agree on why this matters.

It matters because of what we do with the info. What we do with the info is what matters. Not the info blowing a solo. There's a duet we do with commerce. That's the long trail of transactions that record what we buy and sell. Then there are the deeper less chartered areas of human affairs that are non-denominational and largely off-limits to screens, and by extension machines. This is where a search engine under the controls of a capable researcher can prove out an hypothesis, break open a case, or throw long-settled arguments into doubt through new ways of looking at established evidence. Yes, this stuff truly matters.

Information is not always static. Often it too takes actions through behaviors that may still sounds abstract to our ears. This abstraction is about to get real. This book introduces practical approaches for effectively managing online information. This is news for those of us who were never shown how to judge its quality or blend it into our fact-finding or conclusions. This book is for those of us who weren't taught how to integrate our findings into the recommendations we make when we share our investigations with peers, clients, and the wider communities we serve.

We've Been Had

In this book we will push some assertions that will challenge us and maybe even cause us to push back. Here are two basic premises that have yet to be challenged by students, peers, and clients alike:

1. Most folks like to be useful.

2. No one likes to be "used."

We don't need to boot up a computer to experience the sinking feeling that we have been "used by information." Anyone whose sure-thing stock pick nosedives knows what it's like to be played – even when it's never clear who: (1) the other players are, nor, (2) who the actual culprit is who swindled us in the first place.

However, being on the Internet puts us squarely in the path of an information monsoon that knows no seasonal boundaries. To the novice just asking a question of a search engine can lead to an isolation-fed confusion. As a stranger the same question and our alienation with the machine could become an invitation to share with another person, maybe even strike up a common interest: "Yeah, I'm feeling used too!"

Used by information on the Internet means we have entered the vortex of Internet time. Ask a simple question? Get a convoluted answer! Even if we don't know much about the topic we're searching, the search engine knows even less about the extent of our knowledge! The result is that we are prone to fritter away our time...

■ Trying to find answers to questions, and

■ Trying to find meaning in useless details

Can't digest a gazillion search results at a time? The Internet can swallow our entire day and we can still end up starved for information. How can we force it to respect our time? How can we turn the tables from shopping options to questions answered? How can we nudge our investigation forward towards a set of choices offered in the evidence we turn up, not the ads visited upon us?

This book includes a series of approaches that will prevent us from falling into the black information hole of the Internet. These frameworks will defend us against the perils of exposure to "too much information." That way this surplus becomes a good thing. Not just an idle abstraction.

It's our own knowledge deficits that spark our curiosity to ask questions. How and where we ask them makes all the difference between drowning in a swollen tide of information and paddling to a shore of understanding.

Best of all unlike these impending floods, the book's frameworks are stable and will work for us regardless of the latest changes to the: (1) topics we're tracking, or, (2) the technologies we're using to track them.

INFORMATION BY ITSELF ... HANGS ITSELF

© Fraser Mummery: Noose from The Sex and Death Gallery

It's true that knowing what, how, and where to ask questions of computers is critical to using the Internet effectively. But even more fundamental than these skills is the need to come to grips with the very meaning of what information is.

> *Information to most of us is an abstraction.* **(McCreary, 2008)[1]**

Not only is there too much of it. It bores us to tears with its cryptic, detached nature. Until we lose our shirt in the market, or our identity is stolen, it's hard to define our information-seeking requirements. How do we qualify accuracy? Validate assumptions? Learn from past mistakes? Enlist new methods to stay ahead of yesterday's news? On a personal level most information is not of interest to us.

But what people do with it is a fascination. We don't care what information is called. We care what it does. That's when we're not engulfed but engaged.

Maybe our company is tempted to cut the one cost that we can't – our position. Perhaps we are trying to find a clinical trial of a new medical procedure for a loved one with a quickly-advancing illness. What about finding a way to meet with someone whose expertise or powerful position precludes our reaching out to them? In all these instances, there is a clear risk and tangible reward for knowing upfront the underlying purpose of our investigation.

The risk is that the novelty of our in-boxes distracts us from our pursuits. The reward is that we're not collecting idle facts but piecing them into an explanation, a decision, a plan of action. That's how we know we've steered clear of the vortex. We know what actions we can take once we find what we're seeking.

So now it's back to the hunt. Why are we the ones, it seems, that are being hunted?

FORM: IT ALL SOUNDS GEEK TO ME

That's because most public discussions about using information focus solely on form – how fast is our network? How legible is our screen? How secure is our credit card information? How light, fast, and cool is our latest smartest phone for staying connected to the web 24/7?

Don't get me wrong. Without technology there'd be a lot less information to manage. The latest gizmos, graphics, and cyber-safeguards have their place. But keeping up with technology is not a job that non-techies are either qualified or interested in tracking – particularly when tomorrow's marvels leapfrog over today's advancements at breakneck speed.

On the other hand, learning how to handle the raw, unfiltered flow of information that technology unleashes is a skill that doesn't grow obsolete with the next generation of the latest version. Managing information is a lifelong pursuit. The goals, objectives, and methods for achieving them will be just as valid ten or twenty years from now as they were before the advent of the web or after the next killer app.

The more expertise we have, the more these approaches help to keep us current and informed about our field. Best of all, information management levels the playing field. We are just as qualified to become a capable information manager as the savviest techie – no matter how intermittent our hot spot, wide our screen, or deep our local drive.

Independent of our own needs, there are inherent systemic forces that shape the kinds of information available to us:

1. An environmentalist studies the influence of climate change on displacement of large human populations.

2. An economist examines the interplay of market forces and government policies.

3. A marketer considers the consumer behaviors that belie the latest spending trends.

4. A lobbyist compares the voting patterns of Congressional members with the opinions and sensitivities held by their constituents.

Each mission involves trade-offs, interpretations, case histories, and ultimately the roles and responsibilities that come with decision-making. That said, there are immutable laws and principles governing the supply and demand for information – regardless of the stakes and the turf covered in each pursuit.

Some information flows are cyclical. Other sightings are ad hoc as a need arises or an alarm sounds. Many eventful understandings are reached in the shadows and through handshakes. Other transactions are explicit. They don't transpire without documentation. All of these *form* factors conspire to make information useful or a hindrance. These informational forms instruct: (1) the way researchers conduct their investigations, (2) the way marketers survey consumers, and certainly (3) the way the leaders we elect try to influence public debate of their policies.

An information-savvy researcher needs to know how information is produced. More than that, we have to determine how it travels between message senders and receivers. That's how information behaves, or more to the point – how it changes people's reactions as it reaches them. If we're going to put information to work for us, we need to understand the events, conditions, and observable impacts of online information on our search targets. These are the behaviors of the people and groups that find themselves in differing circumstances, awareness levels, and most of all, how they act on their awareness of those circumstances.

PERPCEPTION: Source Fluency

© Pixabay.com

This book begins with a foundation for understanding what kinds of information are out there. Once we reduce information down to the basics, we'll better know what will ultimately work for us. Work literally means putting useful information to good use.

Those basics are reduced to some simple frameworks for understanding the motives of information givers. That's not simply what the search engine reassembles for us but what publishers *get* in return for making their content available to us.

The skill we will learn in **Unit Three** is source fluency. Being fluent in a language enables us to engage directly with native speakers. So too, becoming source-fluent means finding the right tool and how its proper use makes information work better for us. Better still, we won't be at the mercy of any one source. This is always useful in the fluid and evolving world of digital resources where publishers are looking for revenue models more frantically than we may be looking for search targets. Fluency increases our flexibility to call on information providers that may be pivotal for one search, or become time-honored sources, or fade from view altogether.

SUBSTANCE: Lies, Damn Lies, and Factoids

What are some effective procedural steps for getting the right information? Usually it's the stuff that increases in value once it connects to our own prior knowledge and experience.

Think about it. A piece of information is rarely of interest by itself. These are factoids. They may invoke amusement, curiosity, but not necessarily a call for action. That's called collecting more factoids! It's when we combine information with what we already know that it becomes part of the plan we're drafting, an outcome we're forecasting, a decision we're weighing, a turn of events in our favor.

Given that we have limited time and lots of questions, how do we meet deadlines while sidestepping the obstacles that distract, confuse, or overlook the information mission we're on?

The gateway into online information is the search engine. We will determine through search engine selection what is the best fit for the job-at-hand. Maybe refresh our knowledge on an area we're familiar with? Perhaps we'll land specific details on a case we're working? Like any productive interview, an exchange between us and the search engine requires some preparation on our part.

Preparation for what, exactly?

1. **Absolutes:** Are we attacking the specifics of facts and details? What are the possibilities for precision?

2. **Generalities:** Are we being introduced to a new topic? How broadly or narrowly do we define our topic?

3. **Comfort levels:** Most importantly, how comfortable must we be in order to logoff with the confidence that we can communicate our newfound knowledge? Do we need a few bullets and talking points? Is it our style to whack through the weeds until we're comfortable engaging the experts, witnesses, and members of the communities we seek?

Key to our preparations is a fundamental question: How do search engines work – specifically, how do I get them to work for me? In order to capture those pertinent answers, we need to understand the range of entry points, formats, and points of view presented on the web. These are known as the **Information Types** we'll consider later in **Unit Three**.

Unit Two will introduce us to **Query Formation**. This includes techniques for refining our search questions using operators, syntax, semantics, and unique IDs. Taken together these practices will help us to...

■ Build a consistent, repeatable approach to managing Internet research projects

■ Construct queries that produce specific answers or patterns that address our broader issues and concerns

Before we take action, we should reflect on...

■ Why we are doing this research,

■ Where we might find what we are looking for,

■ What the outcome may be,

■ How will we go about completing our search, and

■ When will we get to it?

The answers to these basic questions will enable us to create a successful search strategy.

PROMISES AND GUARANTEES

© Lars Plougman: Ask.com anti-Google campaign on the London tube

In this book we will unpack the basic ingredients that go into getting our questions answered by a network of computers. The databases of facts, figures, opinions, and imagery which they contain. This method carries with it the following six solemn promises to you, the reader and researcher. Every investigation surfaces its own unique set of requirements and conditions. That said, we offer several unconditional guarantees for how we'll learn together in these pages:

1. **Out-of-pocket costs:** There will be no additional outlays to you. All sources discussed here are either free or premium content available through browser cookies (details collected in the registration process), tax supported sites such as local public libraries, and nonprofit and university websites.

2. **Memory retention:** There will be no memorizing of websites – an impossible task for even the most memory retentive super searcher. We will not need to memorize specific sites or remember exact locations where information is stored and accessed. Because we will not be using rote memory to store things, we will become more nimble about solving the diverse and unique problems that defy prediction or a set approach in solving.

3. **Reality check:** The research pursuits we showcase reflect the routine examples of actual problem-solvers. Our information seekers are not modeled on hypothetical but actual problems drawn from thousands of conferrals with hundreds of clients in my teaching and consulting practice. The practical side of reality-based lessons is that the solutions *plug in* to our daily work-based routines. Beginning in **Unit One** we'll be applying search project management practices to add value to the research efforts of our employer, client base, and/or project team. This makes us more valued as a contributor and more billable as a project consultant.

4. **Tolerance of ambiguity:** A clear commitment does not guarantee any greater clarity in our search results. Ambiguous results require patience and focus. In **Unit Two** we'll explore the refinements we can use to better connect our intentions with the results of our searches.

5. **The virtue of simplicity:** Technology *will* get in our way. There's no dancing around it. We can have the latest upgrades, access to everything, and all the bandwidth in the world. We will still experience moments of loss, anguish, and inexplicable outcomes to the most carefully laid search plans. We will be patient with ourselves. But also remember that technology is there to serve us. It's easy to reverse roles when troubleshooting why an application doesn't function or a page doesn't load. Ultimately it will be better if we step back, breathe deeply, and simplify our search plan. Don't play the blame game. The source of "user errors" is far from obvious for us users.

6. **Dexterity in problem-solving:** There is no single solution to any one search problem. We won't fixate on definitive answers. We won't get attached to any one source or way of doing searches. That source will be discontinued. The method that hit the mark the last time out may hit the same wall over and over the next time. Dexterity and improvisation will serve us over time far better than rote memory and scripted instructions. Because we will become more nimble, we'll not need to subscribe to password-protected information sources. In short we'll save money as well as time.

Here is one last promise or maybe more like a course sanity recommendation. Don't get hung up on the results. Try a little of this and that. See what works. It's not all going to make perfect sense or provide unequivocal responses every step of the way – even after we've had the time needed to absorb all the lessons and draw our own conclusions.

So if you haven't already done so, breathe deeply, let it out, and give yourself permission to not get it all at once. Let it seep in as only time can allow.

The Challenge of Using the Web for Research

Most subject experts approach problem-solving in a methodical way so that the solution gives an authority or client the knowledge they need to take appropriate action.

Now let's turn that question on knowledge-ABILITIES: The capacity we have to put information to good use.

Who would we hire if the problem at-hand was about conducting research on the web? How would we frame this assignment? What goals would we set so that the experts could produce conclusions that inform our future actions?

For ten years I worked in the expert-for-hire industry – otherwise known as the management consulting business. Our clients came to us because they believed their internal operations were faulty. Our consultants recommended improvements to their systems by...

- Seeking out the chief-in-charge (authority),

- Changing the rules applied to its workings (process), and,

- Revising the incentives and penalties connected to the success and failure of the overall operation (performance).

The web throws these rules and structures out the window to the chagrin of many sane, rational minds. There are no central authorities, governing bodies, or regulatory agencies responsible for our protection. Were you expecting safeguards against spammers and scammers? What if those hucksters pay our web service providers in dollars and not spam? That's the cost of free information writ into our virtual identities.

The watchwords are no longer *buyers beware*. Even the most unsuspecting recipient doesn't end up with snake oil in their shopping carts or acquire undesired friends without their consent. Avoiding the pitfalls of hucksters, viruses, and other forms of personal violation is largely an exercise in self-regulation.

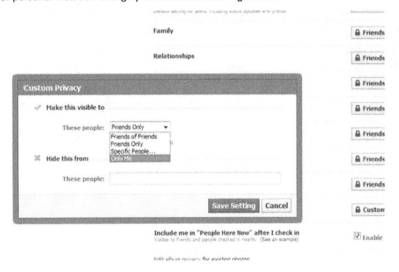

FOCUSING ON REASONABLE OUTCOMES

So how do we penetrate the system called the web to understand the patterns and disciplines that will help us take fullest advantage? Here are the five tenets of reasonable inside the lawless, unrelenting, unsecured vapors of the web:

Faith is the greatest temptation

Stay the Course is only a good idea if we're sure we're *on course*. Loyalty may be a noble trait for standing by close friends and family members. But standing by questionable practices or inaccurate data won't score us points for our steadfastness. Single-mindedness works when we're on a life-and-death mission to find a missing child. But sound investigations do not rest on faith in a pre-determined outcome. It's a healthy disinterest that gets to the heart of the matter. Research in pursuit of a fixed object is dependent on selective evidence. Few have ever hired a "dependent investigator" and perhaps even fewer have ever believed their findings. Pretending we're in control even when we're not renders us both mistake-prone and dense, i.e. failing to learn from them.

Thou shalt not distort, delay, or sequester information

You can drive a system crazy by muddying its information streams. You can make a system work better with surprising ease if you give it more accurate, timely and complete information. We will weigh this factor when we address quality control issues in assessing search results, websites, and even individual pages in **Unit Three**.

Experts do not invite clarity

An honest message giver should not be blamed as the bearer of unwelcome news. Sometimes, however, the message delivered by experts focuses more on their expertise than what it means for your next move. You will have to penetrate their jargons, integrate what they tell you, recognize what they can honestly see through their particular lenses, and discard the distortions that come from the narrowness and incompleteness of their lenses. Remember, sorting all this out is our expertise, not theirs.

The devil is in the over-simplification of details

There is much riding on the desire for closure. There is a constant temptation to simplify the presentation of the evidence you find. Yes, a certain level of order and predictability exists in the world. Some generalizations are useful in ordered circumstances. But this tendency to favor resolution can blind us to the very situations we are called in to investigate.

There's something within the human mind that is attracted to...

- Straight lines and not curves,

- Whole numbers and not fractions,

- Uniformity and not diversity, and

- Bedrock certainties for solving elusive, confounding mysteries.

We confuse purpose and objective

The web encourages the common and distracting tendency we have to define a problem not by the system's actual behavior, but by the lack of resolution it offers. We find it hard to divest of prior commitments that may have outlived their use: We tune out novel approaches and wholesale changes. We mistake symptoms and causes. We obscure the difference between words and deeds, between real experience and imagined metaphor:

> *"The candidate is locked in a war of words, fighting for their political life."*

We can't surge forward with certainty in a world of no surprises. But we can expect surprises, learn, and even profit from them. We can't impose our will upon a system. We can listen to what the system tells us, and discover how its properties, and our values, can work together to bring forth something much better than could ever be produced by our will alone.

Like any computer-based network, the Internet has the ability to match precise outcomes, flag imprecise ones, and calculate. Search engines have learned to synthetically stitch word patterns together in a way that discourages intuition. Websites do not synthesize the selective intelligence we would otherwise expect from the expert for hire. The Internet does not factor in our...

> *"Full humanity – our rationality, our ability to sort out truth from falsehood, our intuition, our compassion, our vision, and our morality."* **(Jucker, 2014)**[2]

It is with a firmer understanding of what the web cannot reasonably provide that we use it to achieve an outcome that only we as knowledge-seekers can deliver.

Marc Solomon
Summer, 2019

---

[1] Lew McCreary, "What Was Privacy?" Harvard Business Review, October, 2008

[2] Rolf Jucker, "Do We Know What We Are Doing? Reflections on Learning, Knowledge, Economics, Community and Sustainability," Cambridge Scholars Publishing, 2014

UNIT FIVE:

HOW TO PRESENT WHAT WE LEARN

IN TEACHABLE WAYS

Investigation as Performance

In the first four units we have reviewed query formation, search mechanics, and some useful models for knowing how and where to address your research efforts. **Unit Five** addresses the more interpretive aspects of the research process. The analytical techniques we review here cut across all the various tools, sources, and commands we have addressed in the realm of web-based search. In fact, the analytical methods we introduce here can be applied in a larger context to your career and even more broadly: The lifelong ability to make sense of an often perspective-resistant world.

IN THE PAPERS

We don't act in isolation. And we don't act before we analyze. And we don't analyze without information that clues us into the implications of our actions:

> 1. What's different about our case?

> 2. What's similar about everyone else's?

It all boils down to conformities and exceptions: How do we stand out? How do we fit in?

The same questions apply to the information we seek for our clients, our families, our social networks, and ourselves:

> 1. How do my search projects validate, augment, or conflict with what I knew before I started?

> 2. How do my new understandings influence the people and groups I need to inform?

Unlike the searches we do, the pages we visit, and the content we stream or download, the value we derive from these collection efforts resists any kind of standard *value add*. We are no smarter or further along based on the volume of keywords, web pages, or research hours we burn on behalf of our research objectives.

Nevertheless, we don't need to become super searchers, let alone mind readers, to draw some universal appraisals:

> 1. What's analysis without consultation? Let's ask our trusted advisers for second opinions about our first impulses. The initial whim to see ourselves as conspiracy victims or crowning victors is how our egos attempt to boost our personal stake in the outcomes of our search results, and the big, impersonal worlds they represent.

> 2. A *gut check* from advisers and friends can preview the impact of our pending actions on the outside, measuring personal contributions within the larger communities we value.

3. This rationale applies as much to the business community as it does our personal affairs. Most of us don't buy stock simply because we think the company deserves our dollars. We buy because we think that others will soon act on the same whim, and nudge our net gain upward.

4. Analysis is inherently social. It is not limited to personal gain or self-discovery. Public perceptions and peer pressure inspire our analytical drives as much as any personality traits or naval-gazing tendencies. There's only one problem for us Knowledge-ABLED investigators. Web search does little to advance these research goals. Social media, with its commercial agenda and feeble search tools, offers even less.

UNIT FIVE LEARNING OBJECTIVES

Let's take a glance back at the foundational settings from **Unit Four** that will be foundational to the presentations we'll be building in **Unit Five**:

■ We considered the guiding principles of group-based information – how the need for group discipline compromises personal loyalties and public credibility.

■ We assessed individual-based information – including the sincerity of personal communication, its predilection for authenticity, and the limitations of its candor.

■ We used common social media platforms to contrast the roles and priorities of individual and group site members.

Unit Four enabled us to master the motivations of content producers who use the web as their primary distribution. In effect, we can address the most important and elusive piece of the search log collection method we first introduced in **Unit One**. Topping of the list: Why information providers supply the material we access through digital research tools and methods.

Understanding this is critical to the fundamental goal of the Knowledge-ABLED. Not only the quality of these materials, but how they inform our cases: The recommended actions to take from our investigations.

Upon completion of this unit, you should be able to present your findings through the following three stages:

1) Analysis and Report Delivery

■ Select appropriate presentation methods to map findings to follow-up actions

3. Use the metrics introduced in **Unit Four** to assess the volume and nature of attention paid to the case and the broader policy issues it addresses

2) Search Project Integration

■ Join a social network and conduct background searches and interviews

■ Map discussions to community awareness and broader public deliberations

3) Presenting the Results

■ Present the final search project

■ Project components (including project setup, search logs and conclusions/recommendations)

SEEING THE WORLD THROUGH THE PERSPECTIVES WE RESEARCH

How do we give life to idle facts?

How do we define the marketplace of ideas, the radar of public awareness, or the boundaries between common knowledge and inside information?

We need to see our activities in context, not isolation. Corporate librarians and professional researchers are still called upon to scour premium databases for marketplace changes. But without analysis, this is a latent function of marginal value, or enduring interest.

Worse, to the people who don't know us (say, our boss's boss), subscription databases are an unrecoverable expense. Market watcher OVUM Research makes this point:

> *"Very few individuals are able to generate business value from the act of searching for information."*

There is no value, not without connecting external situations to internal implications. Not without weaving a common thread between events running their course.

The purpose of news creation is to inform. First, we focus on who did what to whom, where, and when (the core details). Then comes the speculations over why (opinions and commentary). Now apply that formula to today's Times – then to tomorrow's Journal. How much of this is what happened yesterday? How about last month? The wires have already filed those stories.

Day after day, stories are filed that focus on coming weeks or prior quarters. Major media sources cannot republish restatements, or they too risk becoming the publisher's worst fear: *Yesterday's news.* A Biggest Picture perspective enables us to frame the context of marketplace changes for any client so they can better understand the fundamentals:

What the news means to them

.... as well as how this helps them develop their own media strategies:

What they mean to the news

Put another way, external monitoring cuts two distinct ways:

1. **The opportunity:** How do I get my name *out there* (by standing out), or

2. **The risk:** How do I protect my good name (by fitting in or just lying low)

Offering this perspective means looking at the practical considerations of market realities through the client's eyes:

4. **Limelight:** Are we the center of attention – on the periphery, off radar completely?

5. **Influence:** What's the prevailing wisdom – who carries the most sway?

6. **Control:** What seismic shifts are beyond our grasp – what's within our resources?

7. **Momentum:** How do we set the agenda so that rivals are on the defensive?Unlike the examples in the **Unit Four**, momentum is not the sole province of misinformants!

These are not theoretical quandaries. These calculations factor into every marketer looking to gain executive approval, or internal decision seeking to curry market favor.

The media is full of assumptions. This conventional wisdom is based more on convention than astuteness. These are sweeping conclusions that fit the narrative of a particular commentator or viewpoint. Such posturing is common, rarely questioned, and sounds something like this...

■ When are moments 'defined'?

■ Where are careers 'made'?

■ How are reputations 'shaped'?

■ What are the 'best-known' 'best known for?

These parenthetical questions are answered squarely in the gut, not in the head. It's the smaller picture perceptions we all know. Yet we extrapolate them to contain the same known universe we commonly accept as the marketplace, the business world, the competitive landscape, etc.

Another downside to gut checks is that they wear out their welcomes. There are no numbers to pad seat-of-the-pants decision-making. So there are no results to test the impact, and the need for re-sets and adjustments. It's not that marketers shy away from facts and figures. It's that no one knows quite how to measure bloated search indexes, unaccountable sources, and competing points of view.

These are vestiges of information glut, a condition that impairs our clients' ability to be well-informed. Without the bigger picture, it also threatens our status as knowledge providers to others. It overwhelms organizations with news developments they are not neither prepared to exploit or avoid.

It guilts them into an obsessive drive for detail that causes the loss of perspective (and valuable time) in the process.

Internal policies aside, the success of our digital investigations hinge on this Biggest Picture perspective: How campaigns are received beyond the marketing teams who conceive, approve, and execute them.

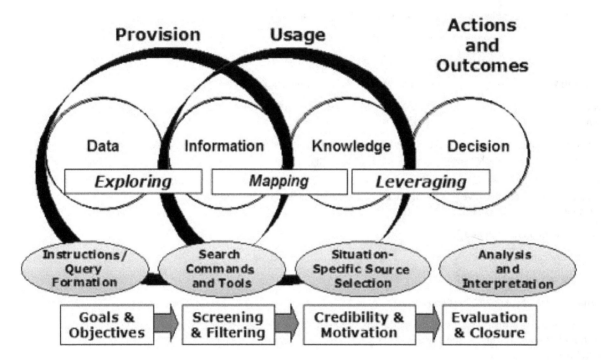

Along the Knowledge Continuum we are now in the evaluation and closure phase of the knowledge continuum, prioritizing the quality information we deem worth acting on or advising as part of a larger decision process.

<u>**Unit Five Destination: How to Connect What We Learn to Useful Outcomes**</u>

Unit Five takes us from the w*hen* to w*hy* steps of the SPM process. That means that we're finally ready to connect dots, draw conclusions, and offer advice. These are the recommendations supported by the evidence we've collected and filtered in **Units One** and **Two**, and analyzed in **Units Three** and **Four.** Each time through the explanatory power of Knowledge-ABLED models and frameworks.

We talk about opportunities when we use information. We think in terms of risk when others do so. **Unit Five** focuses not only on what we learn but how this works in relation to what others know and perceive. How can we as messengers assess the nerves we strike, and the buttons we push — the impact of our research.

The first four units focus on how to gather information and act on it. **Unit Five** is about how others will act on the research we deliver. How will these responses resonate through social media? More formally, how will they play out through reports and presentations to peers, clients, and other audience groups? How will our findings be interpreted and acted on? They key is in the how: *How* we deliver them is every bit as important as the presentation itself.

Unit Five brings together the search project management steps, query formation, quality controls, source fluency, and information conjugation methods to deliver our research to the clients, colleagues, and communities we're supporting. Our presentation methods will demonstrate to our project recipients how our informed use of web research tools and practices is bringing value, economy, and even closure to complex and resource-hungry investigations. Then we turn our attention to the report itself. The presenter has come to grips with the news being delivered, the sense-making of their analysis, and the changes they're proposing. That dynamic forms the core of **Unit Five**.

How our findings are interpreted and acted on is perceived through three common reasons why our audience will be captivated by the presenter:

> **1. The Powerful:** We focus on those who control our destinies in order to know what to anticipate. This is research done about those in authority that our attendees don't know personally or deal with directly. Predicting what will happen and when is the first step towards turning the recommendations we provide into the actions mulled by our stakeholders. **(Sutton, 2009)**[1]

> *The powerful – People pay attention to those who control their outcomes in order to know what to prepare for and when it will happen.*

> **2. The Explainable:** Insight and validation so that we know we're not alone. That through coordination and planning, we can accomplish mutual goals. A strong presenter doesn't assign blame or issue all-or-nothing ultimatums, but posits a range of options that the audience desires. All are practical considerations, preferably choices where stakeholders are predisposed to committing the resolve and resources to see it happen.

> *The explainable – Insight and validation to potentially influence outcomes in our favor.*

> **3. The Unexpected:** Change is hard. Making the right adjustments depends on avoidance of the number one threat to our control – complete surprise! Nothing grabs the attention of our audience faster than hearing what we didn't expect to happen during our investigations. Nothing focuses the mind more sharply than reasoning how to handle changes on achievable terms.

> *The unexpected – Humans react negatively to unexplained events. The tendency is so widespread that it's preferable to give a negative reason than none at all.*

Unit Five Benefits

Unit Five shows participants how to proceed from the analytical to the presentation phase of their search projects. These are the conclusions that us Knowledge-ABLED investigators reach in order to inform clients, decisions, policies, and the communities worthy of our involvement, concern, and influence.

At the close of **Unit Five**, we should be able to determine what to include and discard. We will determine compelling ways to present the findings and recommendations informed by the contextual factors evidenced in prior units — namely PCF ("Provider Conjugation Framework") and VOI ("Vectors of Integrity").

Our allegiances are personal. The methodologies we consider in **Unit Five** are anything but subjective. But we aim as presenters to stand above the preferences and loyalties of any specific influencer: Be they information provider, digital marketer, or web researcher. They are presented as a means to transcend the limitations of self-referential assertions and individual biases.

We'll learn how to eliminate the guesswork for determining source selection, query formation, and the kinds of questions answered by **The Biggest Picture**. The Biggest Picture ("TBP") is a data-driven and repeatable way to quantify media perceptions of events, issues, and campaigns. While the results are repeatable and fixed, the target we're scoring is a moving target. Such are the outcomes wishing to be achieved, rivaled, or avoided altogether by our TBP clients.

We saw in **Unit Two** how SEO ("search engine optimization") decodes the keyword patterns in the top-of-mind associations of Internet users. In a comparable way, TBP models what information providers supply in the way of...

- Topics,

- Relationships, and

- Even explanations for connecting news with newsmakers.

The results drawn by our Biggest Picture provides a narrative for walking clients through their own best intentions and worst nightmares that live at the behest of the external world.

Searching Out Loud

SECTION 5:1 | Quantifying Knowledge–

The Survey-Making Nature of Internet Search Results

"My toaster is more powerful than my computer ... when it comes to making toast."

– Stephen Landsburgh

THE BIGGEST PICTURE

Think of search engines before you started to search out loud. Think of how you may have googled without factoring in some query formations of your own making? That's the level of competence we expect from our layperson search peers. They don't delve further than top-of-mind keywords. Therein lies an unsettling question at the core of the most innocent query: How far down do we submerge before we've settled a score, arrived at a decision, or exhausted a topic?

It's that difference between what we uncover, and what a casual user experiences from that same block of research time. That difference is important for two reasons:

1. It helps justify the time we spent investigating – especially when we're billing that session back to our clients.

2. It helps us anticipate any notable gaps in awareness between surface landings and our deeper excavations.

The second point is absolutely critical to unraveling the greatest mystery in the delivery of any consulting service. The suspense rarely lies in what we're delivering. It's how our delivery pushes on one sensitive button: (1) What the client already knows, and (2) what they're hearing for the first time.

If we're unsure, then the chances are much greater of *showing them up* for not being *in the loop* or *in the know*. Even worse, we can presume that clients don't need filling in or a fuller context because (1) they're too stressed already to absorb more details, or worse, (2) that they know it all cold, and that their preconceptions are as immutable as the facts we're revisiting together.

Airtight interpretations

Many of the deliveries we'll be making in **Unit Five** are shaped by what that client is prepared to receive. That's valid whether (1) we've found eyewitnesses that will testify on their behalf, or (2) that a loved one is suffering from a life-threatening illness. Whatever arrows are carried in our quivers, we need the evidence gathered to be accurate and timely. But it also needs vetting for its credibility, authenticity, and perspective. That kind of presentation is not referenced in any search sites or web pages. It's the meanings derived from our findings that draw clients into the often anxiety-ridden zone of acting on a pressing decision.

Our interpretations don't need to be airtight. Giving our imaginations, license to explore is granted by the fact base of our investigations. Factoring in the motives of our information providers is a tool to help our clients form their own opinion, or gauge their agreement level. They may conclude differently, but it will be based on the same evidence, and understanding about the sources who provided it.

<u>**Organizing Principles**</u>

Content analysis means taking a sample and measuring it in the aggregate. This is in much the same way a survey measures the pulse of collective opinions. It hasn't gotten any harder to collect samples through the web. What's difficult is ascribing motivations to specific editorial communities within those content groupings. Assembling news in the mass media period meant that certain rules and customs were followed. Guarding a news division from charges of libel or slander was an operational necessity for all publishers, no matter whose reputation they were denigrating, or higher truth they were defending.

There are no longer these shared motivations across the political spectrum for defending these First Amendment freedoms. In today's climate, it's hard containing one agenda to a specific website, let alone a region, an ownership ring, or a media genre. Regardless of vested interests and political persuasion, how can we hope to apply uniform standards across the board? We don't factor in every public company to determine how well the market performed today. We don't poll every voter to forecast an electoral outcome.

So where do the **Vectors of Integrity** kick in if we're gauging moods and detecting trends? We need a survey sample that's representative of the whole, not the definitive word on every last news source. That's how content analysts can answer these concerns: Navigating the sources that others find too voluminous to organize, and too jumbled to navigate.

SCORING FORMULAS

The world's message supply is unlimited, and will only expand as the web becomes more *worldwide* or fractures into spheres of influence. But all those messages encounter a fixed number of waking hours. Attention divides where messages compound. Here's the formula:

> ***Attention Supply ÷ Attention Demand = Message Value***

Start with the total content supply or story counts as the baseline. This helps determine how the media world parcels out its cumulative focus. Let's break it down.

<u>**Attention Supply**</u>

You would think everybody in the public arena wants attention. Honestly? Let's consider how most organizations go about trying to acquire it. Each advertiser boasts about its stature. Each company proclaims to be a market leader. Have you heard this all before? We may have never visited their website, downloaded their app, seen their ads, or heard of their products. And we can still recite their goal of world conquest without remembering the details for how they get there. That's because our ears glaze over from every press dispatch ever released in the annals of publicity-seeking.

Press releases, for example, try to confer authority and status on the same people who approve them. Before social media, they were ridiculed outside the PR trade as self-serving, delusional. That assumption surfaces whether the information provider is communicating about themselves or not. Such are the perils of open platforms and publishing on demand.

Press releases were always seen as literate spam – an orchestrated way to stage a one-way public conversation. Even today, they're an accurate way to assess how organizations see themselves in the milestones they find worthy of announcing:

1. Who are their most prized customers?

2. Who are their most valued contributors?

The external side of internal recognition is critical for assessing how strongly those messages permeate and are reflected back or even shared at all by the wider community.

Attention Demand

Face it. The market does not care what a company thinks of itself. But it may devour information on what sets that company apart – if it comes from someone outside the company. Whatever the reaction, verdict, or decision, the response will be delivered via demand-based media. The impact will be measured in the differences between push and pull: Supply and demand-based media.

In the former, supply-demand cycle information suppliers would peddle their wares to their editorial customers. News and feature editors would *buy the argument* that at least some of these noisy, boastful press releases contained (1) information their readers wanted to see, and (2) that it was worthy of their attention. It was believable, at least once it saw the light of day in print.

Fast forward to today and credibility is still the lifeblood of reporters, analysts, and public leaders. At least in any field where success hinges on the ability to speak plausibly, to and for one's peers. This is the essence of PCF-based group identity. This is what we introduced in **Unit Four** as first, second, and third party provider conjugation.

The same holds true for our survey sample. We need to establish source credibility as we shape our demand media sample. We'll be doing so by piecing together the coverage patterns of disinterested third-parties. That primary motivation remains reaching the widest audience, not in carrying the narrowest message.

Message Value

Think of message value as our credibility gauge. Message value is critical if our client's executive or marketing team is concerned about protecting assets, gaining traction, or just plain campaign success. Here a TBP perspective can cast a clarifying light on these otherwise murky calculations.

Message value hinges on the extent that third parties (bloggers, journalists, op-ed editors, pundits, etc.) cite the search target in our media sample. We arrive at message value by dividing attention demand into message supply:

1. The greater the content supply, and the less the media demand, the lower the message value

2. The lower the supply, and the greater the demand, the higher the value

Another way to frame high message value is to determine how little *push* is necessary to sustain the most *pull,* or gain the most traction. It is one calculation in a series of analytical ratios to measure the heavy, often unforeseen hand of external pressures, and influences of the marketplace.

MANAGING THE PROJECT

For years, managers of all stripes have exploited standard operating procedures ("SOP") to measure corporate performance. The rationale is this: While all organizations are unique, each competes for attention, resources, and revenues or funding in 'lines of business' or services with 'layers of management' or operations.

Here's what's not so rare. Relationships are formed between *vertical* industries and the *horizontal* functions filled by the organization's employees. Those bonds contain a finite set of arrangements and outcomes. These are interactions between the organization and marketplace that unfold over a business cycle, or a social calendar.

How stable or transitory a period are our clients cycling through? Set up a query that monitors management changes over quarterly periods. Just how sleepy a lull or tumultuous a shake-up can be quantified. TBP applies a consistent method for addressing horizontal business functions over a fixed time interval, and set of information providers (demand media).

The content supply is the total number of these interactions. Tracking them is a fixed number of messengers – that's our demand media grouping. They assemble a finite set of outcomes (speculations and results) from a menu of milestones (staged and unplanned events).

SETTING UP THE MODEL

Measurement standards can emerge from this Biggest Picture method for rating the market presence of organizations and the nature of their public identities. That's a broad perspective. But the model can also focus on more precise impacts:

1. The record of a specific business unit within a company,

2. The consequence of a leadership change, or

3. The impact of a recent merger on the overall brand, etc.

Conversely, the search target can shift to the internal impact of an external event, i.e. the repercussions of a high profile law suit.

The best way to answer generalities with specifics is to draw a content sample within a meaningful timeframe. We can then parse the sample by how the content addressing our search target collects inside content sources, industry segments, and management functions. We can establish who discusses our search targets, and the intensity of that discussion, by understanding how the model captures these outputs.

Looking for Relationships

Secondly, we'll want to mine those same outputs for bloggers, reporters, analyst organizations, and content-producing channels who contribute(1) the bulk of coverage volume, and (2) the 'opinion weight' about our search targets. Opinion weight determines whose influence tracks most closely to the transcendent themes, and issues surrounding the public identities of target organizations.

It's one thing to measure indiscriminate hit counts. It's quite another to score the influence and impact of public debates, issues, campaigns, and relations. That's why knowledge of content sourcing is critical for assembling a TBP-based content analysis. It equips us to assess the strength of marketing affiliations and the antagonisms formed in public clashes. That's because we can track the size and scope of the content providers that cover our targets and weigh-in on these topics.

Such an analysis can draw a complete picture of an organization's stakeholders and social networks. One that deviates dramatically from the carefully scripted first party communication of a company website, press release, or annual report.

<u>Telling the Story</u>

Content analysis frameworks like **The Biggest Picture** define relationships by translating transactions into story lines. A sound methodology assures our clients that they can be market listeners as well as leaders. Their vested interests won't skew the sample we've assembled. Conversely, the sample can suggest remedies and next steps if the results reveal problems that were otherwise dormant or unaddressed.

Most of us are familiar with the sports metaphor of the 'corporate playbook' for implementing organizational strategies. But the content analyst augments this with a storybook for telling the narrative of the study to the client:

1. Stories create message retention, generating interest in themes and affiliations beyond the main target.

2. Stories 'unfold' – keeping our clients riveted to the next unforeseen or continuous plot twist.

3. Stories clarify the complexities of conflicting numbers and create the consensus necessary to initiate, mend, extend, or dissolve all kinds of relationships.

4. Stories compel their listeners to action – honoring this newfound consensus and the deadlines these decisions entail.

Think of our own organization's fortunes. In corporate marketing it goes something like this:

Quarterly plots consist of a sequence of events or actions that move the story forward by introducing conflicts (say, competing product launches), adding complications (changes in the management ranks), and providing resolution (winning new business).

That sounds repeatable and formulaic. Now how come we can't get Google to connect these dots for us? The problem isn't in our skills as storytellers, or business analysts, but in the garbled way we piece our narratives together.

WHEN CLIENTS COME KNOCK-KNEED

We need to consider this: We resist the temptation to start counting before we can deliver credible numbers about a company's reputation.

First things first. We ask ourselves: What flurry of events would conspire to have a CXO or a marketing genius, or the agencies they retain seek outside counsel about...

- Something they know a lot better than us – their organization

- Something they are powerless to prevent – an encroaching set of unfavorable conditions

Weathering a crisis is the only kind of climate worthy of adaption. To do this may require nerves of steely resolve, and unblinking acceptance of one's faults and frailties. But it absolutely means grounding where an organization has landed to other hardship cases. Such comparisons invite baselines and benchmark evaluations long before an opportunity for the group to regain their footing and eventual stature. It takes numbers.

Here are a few assumptions we can make:

1. The group in question is either under attack, or expects to be within a rapidly closing window of safety.

2. Fear of *where this can all lead* is impeding the leadership from behaving responsibly and working things out as a group.

3. The executives believe they will become the butt of talk show monologues and that they will be blamed for circumstances far beyond their control. Write this off to the conceits of paranoia: Good or bad, it's all about me. Especially the bad!

Insiders like our business leader cracks the door open for outsiders like us during a crisis. Crisis counselors are in the reassurance industry. Executives pay to be told that their darker instincts are clouding their judgments, and that it's not the end of...

- The world they have known,

- The business they've built,

- Growth they have promised, or

- Distant horizons they envision.

But their need for reassurance needs to rest on facts – not on our abilities to console or placate them.

This is where a little perspective goes a long way. A baseline that compares the current predicament to pre-crisis levels of scrutiny and exposure is the first step. This is the foundation for understanding thresholds, precedents, and anticipated trends. That's where the reassurance can begin. It's what the client should expect should the crisis run its course. Perhaps that includes some preemptive moves which could accelerate the healing process or resolution of the crisis.

Once the pre and current baselines of client media coverage are established, the same sample sizes will need to be scoped to the topic in question. Our first use case features the before and after effects of a high profile lawsuit filed against a national food chain on grounds of misleading consumers (target crisis). *Note: Unit Six is a use case that plays out where we, the Knowledge-ABLED, are both the consultant and client.*

UNIVERSE OF CLIENT

Cyclical tracking is useful for determining a baseline of news coverage and comparing crisis periods to more benign news cycles. Firestorms come and go. Search targets will forever be staked to standard time frames.

FIGURE 5.1: All Mentions of Taco Bell in Google News for the First Half of 2011

Note the custom range parameters in the box on the lower left. Date ranges are essential for creating a meaningful sample for applying a 'Biggest Picture' analysis of a search target's media exposure.

Universe of Topic

Next, we need a handle on the larger pool or context that frames the organization's mission, business segments, stakeholders, and communities of interest. This sample ensures that the actions and outcomes discussed in the media are addressing a major policy or public concern of interest to our search targets and/or clients.

FIGURE 5.2: All Mentions of Food Safety, Poisoning, or Food Contamination

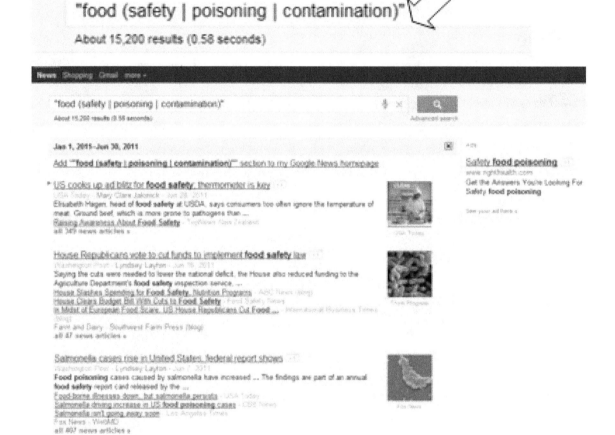

This results page represents Google News for the first half of 2011. Note the usefulness of semantics in the form of word algebra for generating a targeted range of outcomes from which to test the public standing of the search target (Taco Bell).

Cross references

We note very little overlap when we merge the topic and client samples. Does that mean Taco Bell is rarely mentioned in the same breath as food safety concerns? Yes.

Does that also mean that our search target is in the clear, regarding public health concerns and its menu of products? Absolutely not.

This is the stage where we need to analyze the cross references for clues about where Taco Bell's reputation can be further compromised. Just because little coverage is generated in our topic universe doesn't mean related issues are not in play. It's also conceivable that Taco Bell's products may be implicated in other controversies.

FIGURE 5.3: Cross Reference of Client Mentions and Topic Universe within Same Timeframe

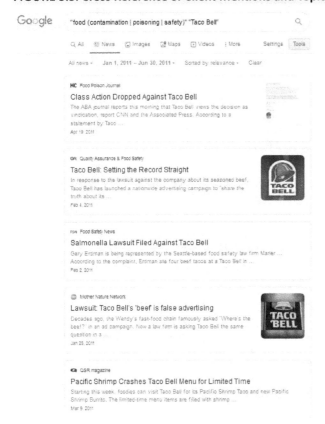

PARTING THE CLOUDS OF JUDGMENT

Nothing scrambles our perspective more than a judgment clouded by preparing for an attack, a siege mentality. If one's guard is up, so are the distortions in our mirrors, and sense that we need to marshal our powers of self-preservation.

The Biggest Picture creates a statistical framework for calculating the extent of that attack both as a looming possibility and as a foregone conclusion. The fact that it's possible to slide between prologue and postscript is a simple framing of the time intervals we're sampling through the date range feature modeled in Figure 5.1.

Beyond analytics and reporting, being able to test past history, track current trending, and hypothesize around future scenarios has another positive impact. That's the ability to add perspective to clients inclined to inflate their impacts, both pro and con, on the markets they serve.

Conversely, as a participant, this broader perspective can breed more engagement than detachment. Tracking scores unfold. Clients ponder what finer points to cultivate, tweak or even trash: A Market heats up, a crisis winds down, a theory runs its course.

It's a fairly common consulting tool to benchmark a standard business practice. This is so the client can assess their relative standing among their peers. Their relative stature determines where to *raise their game*, or alternatively, to recede back *into the pack.* For example, "here's how you're doing on eight dimensions of risk" is just the kind of value proposition that a benchmarking outfit will pitch to the leadership of an operational function within a larger organization.

This kind of orientation is the performance measurement fare we'd expect to see in assessing the internal productivity of a business unit. What about outside perceptions? What if the weakest link in that same unit's supply chain causes concern about the quality of its products, or the legitimacy of its services? Such doubts can ripple through the longstanding reputation of well-established brands with undiscriminating haste.

Ironically, those on the receiving end of public scandal are no better informed or reasoned than the customers who move quickly to do business elsewhere. One way to lower the stress level is to conduct a post mortem of a crisis event. Like the more traditional benchmarking of internal functions, a perception-based survey like TBP is a sober, clear-headed, and repeatable way to gauge the after-effects, the settled perceptions in the post event aftermath.

Post Mortems

That post event reckoning is not limited to damage assessments. Counter measures can be just as meaningful. For example, it's a fair question to ask how effective were the responses to an original threat. In the case of Taco Bell, the parent Yum Brands insisted on a public apology in a Wall Street Journal ad. This message was aimed at the illegitimate claims of Taco Bell's detractors.

So what gets measured in this counter-measure? The key indicator is not about the intensity of the resulting press coverage. It was about how the brand's exposure to risk was lowered or not, depending on the shift in the post event numbers.

It's a familiar story. A dubious claim with a speck of veracity arrives from nowhere: Taco bell = sawdust. Freaked-out executives switch to reactive mode. Their tepid responses are tentative and slow. They are the butt of late night talk show jokes by the end of the next news cycle. The top brass circles the wagons:

> 1. We're getting killed – really? Is this how it feels or is that how it is?
>
> 2. Did sales really go down?
>
> 3. Could the same be said of Yum Brands' capacity to absorb the unexpected?

Reference points must be determined and tested before inviting any further comparisons. It's not me and you against the world. It's not within a world where every element is boiled down to good or bad. We need to correlate concerns and interests against other externalities that we'll detail in the next 'Likely Suspects' section. Before we internalize a threat, we need to catalog it, score it, and connect it to a larger playing field of risks and opportunities. Before we determine what scores to settle, we need to establish the scoring system.

We now need to cultivate a range of potential influencers capable of impacting the stakeholders and communities representing or served by the target in question. Sound familiar? These are the groups or parties diagrammed in the PCF.

How do we do this? Before we proceed, we need to better understand this other pre-existing universe.

<u>**Likely Suspects**</u>

It's critical to generate a meaningful volume for determining the baseline or pre-event level of media exposure. But it's equally important to test the nature of the coverage – specifically what connections are being made and the strength of those relationships.

A baseline is essential to calculate the swelling of post event fallout. The nature of the coverage helps us to characterize negative connotations such as the distortions, innuendo, and scapegoats. It can also offer a positive contrast in more favorable coverage.

Those linkages can take many forms. Here's a listing of some reliable associations and the entities they include:

Events

- Milestones
- Cyclical rites (awards, ceremonies)
- Meetings (communities, trade groups, negotiations)

People

- Executives/Owners
- Spokespersons
- Reporters/Bloggers
- Witnesses/Experts

Roles / Responsibilities

- Stakeholders (board members, customers, employees)
- Competitors
- Elected Officials
- Legal Parties (regulators, judges, law enforcement)

Locations

- Venue (sports, entertainment)
- Physical (crime scene, rights-of-way)
- Region (host community, civic associations, town/city boosters)

As we will see, most reporting is less easily regarded as positive or negative. This is particularly true as we factor in the PCF framework and the multiple, sometimes conflicting ways that different receivers perceive information providers and their messages.

HIDDEN ASSETS

The extended circle of likely suspects is not only key for connecting the analytic *dots,* but for deciding which aspects of the survey to communicate in the findings and recommendations. Most organizations wrestle with some universal questions around the ways in which they're perceived within an external context:

1. What attention am I being paid?

2. How do I use that attention?

3. Which of my reputations are by my design?

4. Which ones do the media identify with?

5. What's the bottom-line and how do we measure up?

6. What's the prevailing wisdom and who carries the most sway?

We understand what's worth pursuing in our recommendations to the client once we've mapped our information providers to this wider community of stakeholders. Remember, we will turn up a lot of new connections and under-appreciated associations by keeping our search terms more generalized and action-based. Figure 5.4 showcases how a Biggest Picture approach demonstrates the public strength of our clients' most overlooked jewels.

FIGURE 5.4: Matching Client's Marketing Assets to Benefits of TBP Methodology

Asset	Approach
Branding Properties	Launch impacts, footprints, stature...
Suppliers & Partners	Relationship strength – the companies we keep
Executives/Thought Leaders	Experience quantifiers – (who's who in which and where...)
Experience-Based Promotions	Contests, conferences, awards, perennials...
Message Projection	Aspirations, tag lines, value propositions, endorsements...
Risk Assessment	Protecting the public identity of private or safeguarded assets
Serendipity	Overlooked venues to position core strengths through joint ventures, cross-marketing and under-leveraged equities

Now let's return to that sub-set of food safety stories mentioning Taco Bell.

LOOKING FOR TROUBLE IN ALL THE RIGHT PLACES

Now that we know who's who, we can see set our sights to these wider and diverging perspectives. That means coming up with a more relevant set of topics for tracking Taco Bell.

What it doesn't mean is fixating on specific events or actors who are likely to change or recede as coverage patterns evolve. It's the nerves they strike and the alarm bells they sound that we're looking for here.

FIGURE 5.5: Sample Page from Prior Cross References

So what's in play here? For starters we've got a regulatory entity (the USDA) and an accusation of a code violation by two law firms. This is a complex matter.

The article opens more questions than it answers. We don't know the relationship between the two law firms or even whose interests prompted them to file the lawsuit. Also, in addition to our client and topic, we've got two additional perspectives to consider:

1. Taco Bell franchisees

2. Taco Bell customers

The main concern for us at this point is to create a more meaningful test for tracking public perceptions of our search target. Now an interesting thing happens. We add the four keywords:

USDA | filling | lawsuit | misleading

We keep our target and our time frame and our hit counts soar from 22 to 191. Additionally, nine of the first ten stories on our Google search page cite the original legal action referred to in Figure 5.5:

FIGURE 5.6: Reformulated Query of Cross References

Note that this search was conducted after the half year mark for an event that occurred close to the beginning of the same cycle. This suggests that 'the story has legs' or that the issue is still active.

The same query in 2019. Note that the story counts are missing below the query statement.

But just how important are the actual numbers? How significant is it Google indexes 191 instances of web pages from what it deems news sources over six months that mention both our target and topic?

Not much.

We must connect events to outcomes in order to create valid comparisons and viable conclusions. We must channel this activity around the media exposure of Taco Bell's peers. We must map coverage upticks and downturns to the specific adjustments it makes to address all the market commotion beyond its control.

Unlike internal goals where it's about *making our numbers*, the external side is scoped by non financial metrics. Defining a target's media performance is largely based on benchmarks – peer comparisons that shed light on perceived threats and opportunities unique to the peer group.

MEDIA PERFORMANCE BENCHMARKING

Topical terms are invoked In order to validate each target. For instance, a term set consisting of the terms restaurant, food, chain, or burger means that McDonald's doesn't track the surname 'McDonald.' Now we overlay five negative outcomes for each food chain consisting of: **scandal | controversial | misleading | lawsuit | complaint**.

FIGURE 5.7: Benchmarking Negative Media Coverage through Peer Comparisons

The term 'filling' is omitted from the benchmarking sample due to its specific Taco Bell connotation.

Here are the tallies based on the leading brands within Taco Bell's market segment:

FIGURE 5.8: Benchmarking Scores of Leading Fast Food Chains

Peer Member	Hit Counts
McDonald's	43
Burger King	125
Wendy's	35
Taco Bell	76
Pizza Hut	44

Now again, these hit rates have limited value without gauging the overall footprint each brand carries within its own client universe. We more clearly see the level of negative press each property generates when we add the total counts for each property:

FIGURE 5.9: Benchmarking Scores of Negative Media Coverage

Peer Member	Hit Counts	Total Counts	Negative coverage score
McDonald's	43	7580	0.6%
Burger King	125	4710	2.6%
Wendy's	35	1970	1.8%
Taco Bell	76	1110	6.8%
Pizza Hut	44	1830	2.4%

The results indicate two clear findings:

1. Team McDonald's is the brand to beat – not just for sales, but for the volume and nature of its media coverage.

2. Taco Bell hit a rough patch that began at the beginning of the reporting cycle, and persists throughout the study period.

So, how do we deliver these results to a client, especially when the news is not exactly flattering?

Here are two presentation factors worth considering:

1) Transparency

Transparency is critical. The client needs less to own the process and more to trust in it. That means our clients get the same results we do. This worthy goal is made all the more elusive in the post standardized results page era of filter bubbles. **(Pariser, 2011)**[2] We're not out to impress an opinion-maker, or an audience panel. We're leasing them a model that will deliver the same repeatable answers when they pose the questions, just as we have in **Unit Five**. Now that's empirical transparency.

The emphasis is overdue. The adoption of open and repeatable standards is no longer a luxury we can do without. That's because the more customized the survey, the more questionable the results. Doctored results cast doubt and destroy credibility. Ironically, such surveys have little merit outside the companies who contract to produce them.

2) Quantification

Media performance is not a direct survey of a primary respondent. It's hit counts – the number of pages matching our search criteria. That's not always clearly understood by the client who may have a more conventional understanding of surveys.

The benefit for them is clear. This is not a new survey methodology, but a quick and demonstrable way to quantify the volume and nature of news coverage. The vehicle is Google, so they are applying a tool they use every day in a deliberate manner.

Another potential point of confusion is that we are using relatively high sample sizes to test subjective versions of a media-based reality. Many business and even marketing folks assume traditional polling methods when one wants to test consumer perceptions. Figure 5.10 suggests ways to communicate TBP benefits to clients, new to media performance benchmarks:

FIGURE 5.10: Merits of Anecdotal Versus Quantitative Surveys

Anecdotal	Aggregation
Qualify	Quantify
Verify	Validate
Consider	Conclude
Speculation	Proof
Squishy	Accountable

Follow-up

Remember the three levels of quality control we explored in **Unit Three**? They include:

1. **Level 1 | Big Picture** – The hit counts of carefully formulated queries used to score the media coverage of search targets.

2. **Level 2 | Street Level** – The site contributing those counts – typically the aggregator or original publisher of the content provided.

3. **Level 3 | Microscopic Level** – This is the actual page within the provider site where the details of the story, the news correspondent, and her interviews reside.

It's time to drill down on the more qualitative distinctions, once the initial benchmarks are established on level 1. Here are two potential next steps for to assess the scoring, and analyze the patterns they yield:

1. In Level Two, source the site roots in order to classify the audience reach and impact of Google News providers. The Wall Street Journal and the Podunk Bulletin & Trading Post may count the same on Level One, but they are not media equals by any measurable standard.

2. Trace the story lines in Level Three that emerge and distinguish what the search engine cannot. This is where the search target is the instigator or main subject (active narrative) versus a bystander or implication (passive narrative). In the case of Taco Bell, think about street crimes reported in the parking lot of a local franchise.

As we also saw in **Unit Three**, sourcing is not just about points of origin, but intentionality: The motivations for informing *who* about *what* that are harbored by all information providers. This is the most dominant factor in our Knowledge-ABLED presentations for two reasons:

1. Knowing the larger social purpose of providing information is the single easiest way to influence its impact.

2. Conferring this to a client is the single greatest value add we can provide, and bill for, as investigators.

THE VIEW FROM BELOW

Up until now, we've been interfacing with the upper echelon. Those are the folks above the folks who sign our checks. Count a fair number who have an ongoing need to know market risks and opportunities. These are the folks in a position to act on them. But it's not all shareholders and venture equity. It's also the folks who pay their bills directly. That means considering the way line managers assess the credibility of their suppliers and bosses. Generally speaking, line managers are the lower level minions who keep operations running smoothly, or retool specific functions to improve those operations. It's this reason our PCF analysis include the internal perspective, not just the market focus.

If there is an inherent bias of using PCF, it's that we're never more than a chance connection removed from testing a theory of hypocrisy and corruption:

1. We all know the first signs that our politicians are not being entirely candid – when their lips move.

2. We all know that banks get robbed because that's where the money is – even by their own bankers.

3. Our powers of BS detection are tested and strengthened each day when elected officials, corporate leaders, and attention-starved celebrities keep three separate ledgers, including (1) their words, (2) deeds, and (3) the difference (a.k.a. hypocrisy).

The journalism industry may never recover. Exposing hypocrisy is as much a winning business model as a self-protective impulse. It keeps our *honest* doubts in line with our *reasonable* expectations.

So how do line managers keep their BS detectors in working order? Let's say they're in fact-finding mode for upgrading the software required to run their business functions. Let's assume there's much to sift through. So much that the volume of pros and cons overwhelms those vows they make to stand their ground.

That position, let's assume, lies somewhere in-between a wholesale upgrade of the latest version, and business-as-usual. Our operations guy needs to see the trade-offs with the options at-hand: To map those choices to their business, their values, their clients. Period.

In the technology business, it helps to bypass the trade show evangelists and seek out those unassuming functional managers. BS levels drop when dealing with working stiffs (like me). That's because operations folks seek not the victory of a sales closing. They crave the solace of living within their system choices.

That doesn't mean anyone manning the booth has a used car they want to pawn off on those walking the hall. But it does mean that the folks who count themselves as payroll costs care more about war stories than case studies. They care about the unexpected experience than the full feature list. They are not looking for outward recognition. They're pursuing the internal approval needed to pull resources and manage their projects.

Those outside vendors will show up on The Biggest Picture radar. Any technology marketer worth their salt is tracking media mentions in trade journals. Preferably, these outlets cater to the function-happy folks and not just to the technology crowd.

Also, that every day experience of the line manager extends beyond reporting structures and project management. It scales not only to her unit and organization, but how that entity is perceived in the wider market. Marketers call this 'brand stature.'

Before we get there, we need to take a step back. Let's review the tools and methods we've already introduced for delivering these Biggest Picture benefits.

INSTITUTIONAL CREDIBILITY

In **Unit Four**, we assessed information context through the lens of two new frameworks: PCF ("Provider Conjugation Framework") and VOI (the "Vectors of Integrity"). These models help us to see the ways our search targets receive and interpret information providers.

We also looked at social information. Here, the perspective of second persons and parties are removed from the path between information providers and recipients. Social media is the most vivid example of this. We then considered the conditions where the coercive elements of misinformation can flourish, true especially where the misinformant is free from divulging one's identity, along with their news.

But what about the messages that are paid for by message providers? What about keywords that are auctioned through the Google Ads program?

1. Do we take a step back as researchers when providers have no other use for us (other than as message consumers?)

2. Do we discredit them because they have the ulterior motive (getting us to buy their products, or sell their arguments?)

Most of us are not such information purists that we must remove all self-serving motives from (1) our search results, (2)database providers, or (3) RSS feeds. But we need to include motivation in the mix when we're sourcing the very evidence we're using to recommend or act on. This question is foundational to The Biggest Picture approach needed to contextualize our search targets. That context covers markets, operations, and stretches over the wider public realm of media scrutiny.

DETERMINING INSTITUTIONAL CREDIBILITY

Here in **Unit Five,** we assess and measure **four motivation levels** used to define credible news-making communications. Each motivate is evaluated according to its surface news value. TBP is there to test the rationales that explain the deeper, implicit understandings between message senders and receivers.

As we saw in **Unit Four**, there are several steps in-between the spinning of *set results* into *net results*. The same dynamics apply whether we apply this to individuals, as we did earlier, or as groups as we address here. In effect, they will learn how to interpret set results based on the guiding principle of credibility. Unclear about the motives of information givers? Look no further than who they're giving out to.

When determining the institutional credibility of a website's content, we need to...

- Anticipate the format,

- Know the media grouping that identifies its readership (local, trade, weekly, etc.), and

- Recognize the sources' self-interest.

Here are three group-based assessment methods available to us.

1) Common interest and word of mouth

One of the clearest ways to define self-interest is to consider its opposite – common interest. A common interest is genuinely forged through conversation, typically between two people sharing experience and advice. Sometimes one person imparts the same with several people. If this form of trusted communication sounds familiar, maybe you're familiar with its marketing identity: Word of mouth.

Word of mouth is a conversation if we reference the PCF model: One to one with common interest. That intimacy is corrupted when that transfer becomes a many-to-one discussion, with a commercial or self-serving first party interest. Think of the word of mouth being swapped out for the word-of-sponsor.

Why do so many institutions rise and fall based on word of mouth? Their success depends on the participation of others, with their time, money and attention. Like the stock market, if a trading system appears rigged, fewer people invest in it. If members of a religious order do not abide by the church's own ethics, fewer people come to worship. Only when we as participants have no other choice is there a public tolerance – if not resigned acceptance – of the institutional corruptions inspired by self-serving behavior. Our longstanding national addiction to oil recalls a lack of choice in America's participation in politically unstable areas of the world. It's a quandary that continues in spite of American energy independence. Astonishing.

One of the interesting aspects in the rise of bloggers and web-based self-publishing is this: Marketers are in less control of word of mouth communications than ever. The many-to-one word from our sponsor cannot compete with the one-to-one word of mouth. A commercial can never be a conversation. We as participants think twice before buying into information that serve the self-interest of companies we do not know, politicians we would not elect, or institutions that have no place in our own value systems.

As information consumers, we understand that the information supplied us on the web is often tainted. Yes, by self-interest but also by institutions posing as *real people* and *trusted advisers*. Such inputs and opinions are swayed, even purchased, by the institutions, corporations and products they steer us towards.

2) Self Interest and media incest

The easiest way to specify something so pervasive and universal as self-interest is to revisit the role of information providers during the infancy of television broadcast:

> *Dateline: New York World's Fair, April 1939.*
>
> *Place: RCA Pavilion*
>
> *"Cue General Sarnoff and action!"* **(Bilby, 1986)[3]**

The first event TV ever covered was the birth of itself.[4]

Love at first sight.

Like all industries, the media's primary business purpose is not to educate, orchestrate or distract but simply to sell more media. Unlike all other industries, the media is entirely comfortable in front of a camera as well as behind one. In how many industries does the annual awards dinner attract a third of all U.S. adults?[5]

The difference between our trophies and theirs is that they don't even acknowledge a camera presence until their acceptance speeches.

So what do we mean about the *incestuous* state of media relations?

One way that the broadcast and cable media is like any other business community is that its members are acutely aware of what each one of them is saying. In fact, stories about media people are easy to deliver:

1. Readily recognized name

2. Little to no background digging

3. Someone whose job security other media folks either want to...

   - Test by questioning their personal choices, or

   - Test by asking for a professional favor

It's all pretty transparent stuff. But like any self-serving fabrication, it's also unbelievable. All the *like this* Facebook approvals can't mask the artifice of backscratching and self-congratulations.

The question isn't who do we believe, when we're all beholden to our own interests. The more interesting problem here for us is to build a rationale. This is the explanation for why and how stakeholders interpret and act on *the news* based on who presents it, and how it's presented to them.

3) Self Importance and media delusion

How do we measure respect?

Every media season witnesses an award overdose. Each year, the industry hands out thousands of trophies at hundreds of ceremonies. Incest abounds as TV broadcasts of Oscars, Grammy and Tony Awards all win Emmys.

Not surprisingly, of all industries the business segment the media is most inclined to cover is ... well ... the media. The self-referential nature of broadcast media is an accepted fact of broadcast content. We expect to hear *plugs* of new books, movies, dieting plans and moral crusades. Self-promotion satisfies the dual need to fill *air* time with the persuasion of coming attractions.

Thus, it's not really news when our media celebrities broadcast their deeply-held beliefs that they are not only informing us, but *speaking for us*. Otherwise, why would they be permitted to hold so much attention within such a public space? The argument for the separation of news-gathering and opinion formation is both world-weary and unwinnable.

Can the two really be isolated? That the self-selection of certain facts and the exclusion of others is not its own form of commentary – a game of tele-prompting through TelePrompTers?

But just because talking heads on cable networks take personal liberties to mold or fabricate our public discourse doesn't disqualify them from competing for our attentions.

Their reputations may suffer. Their influence may wane. But these are addressed in The Biggest Picture model. These are not just nagging questions but receptive to responses. TBP enables answers as calculable as the formulas that aid and abet the delusions we've endured as passive viewers for over half a century.

The Biggest Picture too harbors its own biases. Like most other scoring formulas, it has an implicit goal in moving us from a wider awareness to corrective action. That's prodding our clients to see, understand, and address the kinds of big picture connections CEOs, elected officials, and decision-makers generally make in isolation.

METHODOLOGY

Every survey model comes with its own set of terms and conditions, a.k.a. survey methodology. In addition to statistical ranges of accuracy, a methodology establishes *the how* of the data collection, especially the *how big* size of the sample. Sample credibility for perception measurement is defined by the requirements for painting *the biggest picture.* This means building a successful demand-based content analysis practice.

A demand-based system measures total media attention paid to the issues, commercial assets, and personalities that drive market opinion over months, years and decades. The results speak for the markets – not the marketers. The orientation is based on how stakeholders see the market players. What won't we see in a TBP methodology? How individual companies view their own isolated actions.

Supply media is beholden to the specific aims of a single client function – PR. Want to prove coverage volume is up? You don't need The Biggest Picture to prove out an increase in press mentions. The demand model its based on responds directly to the entire organization. TBP is a reporting and analysis tool to understand and manage the heavy, unforeseen hand of *external factors.* External here is a vague label used to group everything from media hysteria, to crisis communications, and legal counsel.

Defining The Biggest Picture

So how do we put The Biggest Picture into practice?

First let's more clearly define the vision. The Biggest Picture is: a conceptual framework that...

- Defines resonance and context from the fleeting and fuzzy onslaught of commercial messages
- Imposes a structure on horizon gazing – shifts in the competitive environment, management fads and cultural norms
- Creates a numbers-based perspective on non-quantitative information

Now, let's bring it down to daily news cycles and media consumption. We know the feeling of being stressed out by too many incoming messages. We can only assume that information glut once lived the nitty gritty details buried in newspaper text and broadcast noise. The advent of screens in our grasps has exploded the noise level well beyond human cognition. It may sound like the survey-taker would need to barricade such explosions. Actually, instead of trying to contain them, the broadest, breathtaking views can be had from scaling these walls of information.

Problems with Content Analysis

Most content analysis distorts the media it measures by reducing all relevant messages to a simple 'hit count' of pre-considered targets. This is done by polling organizations, market research firms and PR agencies to assess how the media influences public perception of their clients and key competitors, campaigns, events or policy issues. Yet few news stories can be judged as definitively good or bad for a company's short or long-term prospects. It's even harder to shade coverage in terms of *partial* goodness, or *potential* fallout.

Furthermore, predetermining who or what to monitor skews the results in favor of pre-test assumptions. The most sincere, accurate, and credible way to score how these messages perform in selected media is to constrain our analysis. That means limiting the scope of target messages, time frames, and the media they're grouping in.

One must resist the temptation to pre-determine a target company, opinion leader, consulting group, or editorial slant based on a vested outcome. A stakeholder can hold The Biggest Picture up to their own self-reflections. But that mirror image must reflect the same results when a disinterested observer applies the same method to the same sample.

This hands-off approach permits a more credible means to quantify category leaders, media perceptions, message shapers, and the ancillary messages that spin off from the original. It also turns up what we weren't looking for, but needed to find out – a promising indication of useful research.

UNIVERSAL LAWS OF SELF INTEREST

As a PCF analysis indicates, the coverage patterns of news topics by news groupings is far more useful than the first-ten-hits-or-bust approach to conventional search engine analytics. Looking out over the entire provider pool is critical for isolating common stories from unique viewpoints about those developments. In other words, it often depends more on where those search findings are *dropped* than where they're *found.* For instance, who's picking up the tab for delivery through leaks and other backdoor influences.

The universal laws of self-interest apply to groups and individuals alike under the media glare. Credibility, authenticity, and integrity all share ringside seats at the Biggest Picture:

1. Airing one's laundry in public loses credibility, the more the launderer likes to hear their name.

2. A *truth-teller* whose main virtue is their authenticity, think whistle blowers, cannot claim to speak-out as an independent voice.

3. Any witness whose testimony rides on altruism (put group interests ahead of own, etc.) will be discounted, without an audit to determine the personal cost of their admission in blood, treasure, and social hardship.

Post Social Media Fallout

Before the advent of social media, it was easier to define direct from indirect relationships. They were traditional boundaries that separated actors from audiences and primary or firsthand observation from secondary research. Roles played formerly by publishers are less distinctive now that the world can legitimately beat a path to a Facebook page.

So too, the viral nature of social media clouds former distinctions between self and public interest. Connecting to a celebrity's twitter feed is a personified form of self-selection. Membership is not compelled by an overarching duty or requirement to act on behalf of the group for whom one now belongs. The attraction of social media fame could well be triggered by vanity and voyeurism as much as a crusade appealing to a higher calling.

What's the unifying factor that helps us clarify the motivations and behaviors of either extreme? *Self-preservation* seems to have held its breath long enough to outlast most other forms of characterization. That's the perennial force we can use to align information providers with...

- The content they supply,

- The sources they bypass, and

- The ultimate editorial priorities that service their business model.

The Rise of the Web Curator

Supply doesn't drive demand anymore.

It's as true with information as it is with hard goods. The best way to sell in a buyer's market is to not flood the market with more messages, but to figure out the ones being consumed – and acted on.

On the demand side, people don't know their way around much of the information that could otherwise serve them. Accelerating access to news is outpacing people's ability to make sense of it, let alone apply it to their personal and professional lives.

This is not just about consumers but producers. Witness the workspace.

Knowledge workers are pelted with e-mails, interrupted by video chats, and inundated with databases they're blocked from accessing. The insult to the injury here is that any attempts by the outside world to fight to the top of our in-boxes are dead on arrival without a welcoming format. Define attractive? Let's deliver a summary of all relevant data points stakeholders need to gain clarity on their markets, firsthand knowledge on their customers, and, influence in their companies.

This is an invitation for curators to design radars for tracking news flashes and coverage patterns. But it's also an opportunity to harness the explanatory power of PCF to analyze information providers: The *what's-in-it-for-them* equivalent to radars.

That's what we began to explore in our reference to Google Trends, and what we'll refer to as the Knowledge-ABLED framework of a credibility index. This diagnostic spells the difference between...

- Supply-side wire coverage that generates self-proclamations and selling arguments), and
- Demand-side exposure that confirms third party validation and the figurative *buying* of those same ideas.

Trade editors ordain what's news, not just a vendor or PR agency's attempt to create news. The result: An air of respectability is imparted to the *plugged* product or positioning.

The Death of King Content

Every day it becomes more difficult to assess the impact of each competing message. How much of the original message survives? What unforeseen events change the story around? How does one assert authority, let alone authorship, when the story-telling medium is the host to over a billion competing publishers?

For most of the Twentieth Century, an information supplier was a publisher whose most prized piece of hardware remained the printing press, a Fifteen Century invention. Vested subscribers would pay for these paper-based information products – honest! This is a world in which leading publishers bought in to the success of this business model as they grew to believe that...

> *Content is king.*

It meant that select groups of people paid for the information they supplied with their dollars and attention. It meant that the publisher received a double-dip from the advertisers they attract who were chasing the same set of readers.

Content is no longer king.

There is no longer a premium on being the first to know. The future lies in being the first to understand in a way that draws others to that same understanding, (and their own conclusions). That's the manifesto for curators.

Content is a stammering, mucus-laden *umm* among the miscellany of unfiltered search results and anonymously-authored articles in your news feed. In a world where pocket devices are publishing platforms, scarcity isn't measured in speed, access, or being connected, but in making connections. Enter the sense-making territory of the web curator.

<u>**Knowledge Demand = Web Curatorship**</u>

Imagine we're on the exhibition floor of the social media event of the century: Information surplus? Meet knowledge deficit! That introduction is being brokered by a knowledge planner – someone who can reconcile information supply with knowledge demand by anticipating...

- How news travels,

- In what circles, and

- Where that impacts most.

The cultivations of web curators are based on the three pillars of interpretation — context, context, and context. Tell me who said it, who heard it, and where, and what they said becomes immaterial. Tell me the way in which an appeal was made, and the call to action falls by the wayside.

As the PCF demonstrates, show me the eyewitness who lived through the event she's recounting, and...

- We see her authenticity implicitly,

- We infer her emotional investments, and

- This leads us to question her disinterested bystander status.

An accomplished curator is not simply a message interceptor or re-transmitter, but a temperature gauge. This is the pulse taker that assesses the bursts and slowdowns of message traffic within the personal radar frameworks we discussed in **Unit One**.

Nice-to-know works for birthdays and extended voicemail greetings. It doesn't cut it for web searches, where we're operating on a need-to-know-basis. If it lands off radar, it never happened in the first place. Our attentions don't shift.

In this tree-falls-in-the-forest scenario, a web curator is the best defense against the maladies of information fog such as A.D.D., insomnia, the blurring of professional and personal affairs, and disengagement: The anxiety, and periodic paralysis associated with device-enabled availability.

That doesn't mean farming our calendars out to a personal attention manager. That happens in a decade or two. But it does mean answering to the contextual value of our personal mental space: WIIFM ("What's in it for me")?

THE MARKET FOR CURATORS

So how does the curator find their niche? Being all things to all content consumers is about as relevant as trying to bury one's subjective point of view. The new transparency isn't about leveling the playing fields of opinion. It's about linking to sources. **(OnPoint Radio, 2011)**[6]

Unlike the ad-supported models of SEO campaigns, a curator is not a human lynchpin for converting click-happy consumers. Idea people are not buying merchandise. They are buying arguments – those that support the rationales for the advice they sell. Perhaps the killer app here is rediscovering the art of disengagement: Finding no surprises when we reconnect because the curator has our back at all times. Imagine the liberation it gives this over-achieving, insecure, multi-tasking taskmaster:

> *"She tries to communicate a need for balance to employees who report to her, too. "I worry about the speed at which they are going," she says, adding that she wants them to "shut down" when needed, for the sake of their families and their health." (***Meese, 2011)**[7]

Assuming we know what keeps our clients up at night, what kind of radar-building equipment serves the needs of curators?

That's where grounding in advanced search commands and even tired, old traditional media segments come in handy. As we saw in **Unit Three**, using a custom search tool like Google CSE Search to bundle sources, helps to differentiate, quantify, and validate our pet peeves, hot stock tips, and celebrated rumors on the news horizon.

Run those queries in the form of event-based trip wires, and the daily counts form the aggregated patterns of what coverage blows hot and cold. Google Trends runs the media pick-up patterns in tandem with the same terms in Google searches. In effect, we have that same handshake from the trade expo: Media supply meets (or misses) user demand.

These radar constructs are good for high visibility issues that soar and plummet from year-to-year. But many of our search targets would go undetected atop such public radar. For that we need to scale down to a more street level view through localities, community members, and more niche or locally based organizations. That's where an RSS reader like Feed Demon shines as a personalized approach to event tracking and the aggregated coverage patterns – the iPhone equivalent of Google Trends as a personal radar.[8]

FIGURE 5.11: Comparing Content Supply to Knowledge Demand through Google Trends

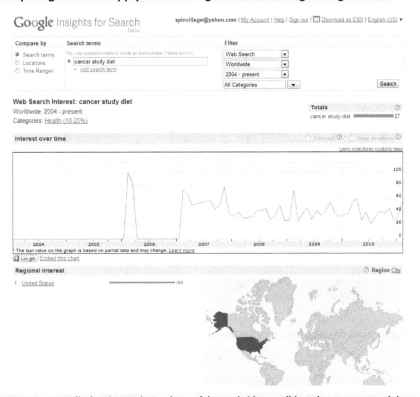

These consecutive screen captures display time series analyses of demand-side or pull-based content sourced through Google's search logs. The web search volumes are then compared in the second graph to the supply-based volumes of media references to the same keywords over the same time period. The latter graph also includes milestones or key events that may have led to spikes in news coverage on the topics in question.[9]

The Value of Curatorship

Finally, curators should sell their quantifiable benefits to a confused and distracted market. That sales pitch starts with single examples. Abstractions like what the best-known are best known for might be a starting point for idea people. For more grounded folks, it boils down to this: One purposeful, unitary artifact that reveals the telling quote, table, framework or footnote – diamonds in the ... umm ... content *rough*.

The bigger picture benefits will emerge once these evidential building blocks become ingrained in our web-based discovery process. That might be sweet music to sleep-deprived crisis managers. It may be a threat as well to the scientists of external risk assessment who traffic in the language of hysteria. This is the paranoid leading the para-blind down an alley of would-be prowlers and invaders. No one likes to depart from the script. No one makes time for interruptions. They arrive unannounced. Their departure comes in its own time.

The impulse to panic is an age-old temptation not restricted to unsuspecting widows or defenseless victims. Is the concentration level thick with anticipation? Is it diffused through false alarms and unmet expectations? Is this...

- A wave of consensus,

- A squeaky wheel,

- A whistle in the dark, or

- A charging stampede?

What are the measured responses that address tangible perceptions – not last night's bad dream but tomorrow's realities, in the light of day?

A curator can discern the strength of association, and tell us where our clients are in their perceived crises. Are they floating near the bottom of a deep-sea, or being washed into shore escorted by the storm surge itself?

These are searches out loud that commercial search engines are not configured to deliver. They are speechless, both in posing the questions, and in tracking the volume and nature of the responses. The old Irish expression is that if you want a crowd, start a fight.

And when our clients do, they'll be needing numbers to back them up, not just attorneys and personal body guards. At the very least, they'll need a web curator who can point out who's in the audience, and why they're there.

Questions Answered by The Biggest Picture

So what are the implications now that we've established a methodology to address content analysis? What are some of the more vexing questions that surround issues of public reputation, perception, and the impact to organizations of largely subjective assessments?

For starters, we remove the 'subject' (the target organization) from the 'investigation' (Biggest Picture methodology).

That objectifies the sample so the results are attributable to sources other than the target. That doesn't mean all media impressions are containable to disinterested observers and non-vested parties. It's still possible that the marketing efforts of the target organization have a hand in the survey outcome. Private interests can rebrand their outbound marketing campaigns as news sites that have no visible tie to their original sponsors. Target organizations can and do hold financial ties to the information providers who cover their activities, or withhold such coverage, depending on their incentive structure.

But The Biggest Picture is not about ownership structures. It's not an under-the-surface investigation. It's the reality of the marketplace perception – an aspect of modern corporate life every bit as skewed as the veiled agendas of political elites, corporate media, and the digital giants.

Choosing Our Battles Wisely

Our target organizations take daily stock of the proverbial news radar. Partly, they're hoping to confirm that positive messages are getting out, and that negative ones don't escape into the headlines.

Perception metrics address the risk factors inherent with crisis communications and market disruptions by determining:

1. What's beyond our target's control and what's within their grasp?

2. What keeps an opportunity open without having to be the driving force?

3. What do they need to know without needing to know it inside out?

The term 'crisis' infers a lack of control over events conspiring to create doubt and uncertainty about an organization's well-being and reputation. It is a gathering momentum that demands an immediate response to preempt further surprises and unexpected market shifts.

It's Always About 'Our' Targets (– isn't it?)

Conversely, questions used to measure market success are wrong. It's not based on what our targets spend. It's based on how they look and to whom. Here's how that perspective-gathering plays out in the context of the wider marketplace perception. *They* in this case refers to how non-vested third parties view our first-party based organizations (and clients).

It's not about...

- The media they place.
  It's about the media they're placed next to.

- The attention they deserve.
  It's about the attention they're paid (whether or not they deserve it).

- The promotions they give away. It's about the company they keep.

- The loudness of their announcements.
  It's about how well they listen for the marketplace response.

- Reaching demographic audiences.
  It's about reaching understandings with the people they want to engage.

- The name they made for themselves.
  It's based on who's introducing them within the forums they address.

Capitalizing on The Biggest Picture

Now let's alter the perception, so that 'they' is now 'us.'

That's the internal discussion we're about to have about acting on the findings of a perception measurement survey:

> 1. What are the questions these results are raising?

> 2. What lines of attack are open? First, for further study, and then for followup?

In a first person plural setting, followup is typically for outbound teams to pursue, including sales, marketing, corporate communications, and public relations.

FIGURE 5.12: First Party Perspective – Connecting Corporate Positioning to Public Perception

COMPARISON	LINGERING DOUBT	BUSINESS SOLUTION
ORGANIZATION	*Are we listened to?*	Reveals sphere of influence status based on our commentator status
	Who is listening?	Vividly quantifies our stakeholders and degree of their stake in us
	Are we believed?	Contrasts ratio of push to pull coverage – what's self-proclaimed and what's conferred
	Are we noticed?	Indicates that our message is out there; how it resonates
	How are we different?	Tests for what propositions have saturated the market and message projection; confirm registering of key differentials
	What's our biggest distraction?	Shows where internal resources are sapped / prone to external pressures
	What's the biggest impact on our organization?	Exhibits dominant theme in terms of internal functions
	Who do people think we are like and in what way?	Capture brand attributes according to the relationships and experiences they connect on
	Are we making an impact?	Weekly movements in perception metrics correlate internal performance goals to the outcome of campaign launches and marketing events

Now let's cast our net beyond the self-referential, and expand it to our stakeholders – anyone likely to benefit or suffer from our market standing:

1. What's the consensus out there when this combination of customers, shareholders, rivals, reporters, and analysts share their collective impressions of what we bring to market?

2. How much are these perceptions justified by the facts on the ground?

3. How much carries forward from past slights, misperceptions, and petty scores not yet put to rest?

FIGURE 5.13: Second Party Perspective – Connecting Market Reputations to Peer Recognition

COMPARISON	LINGERING DOUBT	BUSINESS SOLUTION
PEER GROUP	*Are we a player?*	Tells us how well we compare against established rivals and peer sets
	Is anybody in our space listening?	Reveals gap between aspiring messages and tonality of resulting press and research pick-up
	Is anybody repeating our mantras?	Shows key influencers and their residual off-spin
	Is it being misinterpreted	Shows how detractors dredge up unresolved grievances
	Who else is saying the same thing in our space?	Document leadership status when wannabes try to steal our thunder and cachet
	Who do we think we are associated with and are not?	Compare internal channel relationships with how they play out publicly
	Who is talking about us the most?	Use commentator types to deduce our biggest stakeholders
	Do we command the stature of a company our size?	Alerts us to changes in our week-to-week market presence as well as which organizations or brands exhibit best-in-class scoring by peer grouping as well as overall
	How do our customers see us?	Reveals what media circles we travel in, erasing the blindspots that plague brand-weak organizations who need to better position their products and services.
	Who do people think we're like?	Shows our media distribution by stakeholder

Finally, let's consider saving a seat at the table for strategy. In corporate-speak this is the aspiration-based question we come to once we *make our numbers,* fill a key position, or dispel a rumor. We're over the humps and the horizons beckon: What are those broad strokes or visionary missions that will trigger fundamental market shifts and even summon new ones?

The Biggest Picture can inform tactical choices on our marketing calendars, but its sights are set on helping shape emergent terms and conditions. From a third-party perspective, this means gauging (1) the expansion, (2) maturing, or (3) decline of target markets. It means establishing a baseline for determining the historic intensity of key events that rally and hold the interest of the stakeholders we're trying to attract.

FIGURE 5.14: Third Party Viewpoint – Connecting TBP Perspectives to Long-term Goals

COMPARISON	LINGERING DOUBT	BUSINESS SOLUTION
UNIVERSAL	*What kind of visibility do we want to have?*	Enlists best-in-class brands and overall industry leaders for pace-setting purposes
	How can we stand out?	Lends proof that media distortions warrant changes to our current press coverage
	Who are the cool brands / companies?	Measures category-defiant brands
	What trend can we take full advantage of?	Demonstrate corporate, lifestyle and policy trending from their defining moments to groundswells, herd mentalities and market shifts
	Who is different from us saying the same thing?	Find unexpected friends and adversaries who deliver similar value propositions in unexplored segments
	What space are we associated with that is not our space?	Overlooked markets that suggest a comfortable fit for your natural strengths

SECTION 5:2 | Information Bartering –

When Passwords Fail to Connect

In the days before social media, there was a common distinction between being on and offline. First, we would gather information and then logoff, applying what we learn second-hand from published sources. The subtle difference here is *published* since we could still consider phone discussions or face-to-face interviews with experts and eyewitnesses to be first-hand intelligence-gathering. In pre-social times, we interviewed the computer. We were one step removed in receiving information directly from our intelligence-gathering sources.

But the simple assertion that humans = primary sources and machines = secondary sources holds no longer. Tweeting a celebrity with my blogging homage to their latest album, book, movie, or media tour is not really firsthand or secondary.

Social media has stretched the boundaries of who we touch, while shrinking the effort required to extend ourselves. Moreover, the chance our overtures will be heeded by people we've never engaged directly is no longer a freak occurrence. But we've paid for these additional points of access by diluting the intimacy of our exchanges: Yes I know *of you* but the reference is indirect. It's reliant on multiple degrees of separation, and resistant to our immediate recall.

One constant remains in a world of apps for meet-ups, group gaming, and vocal-free exchanges. Primary intelligence gathering involves information bartering: The act of trading on know-how. This doesn't necessarily mean that money changes hands. Instead, we have information that no one else has – at least no one in the networks where we operate. A capable information broker understands that the value of bartering comes when we trade information to find out what others know (and whether it's our business too!)

Sometimes the trading can bypass the very sources we're investigating. We'll demonstrate one of the least risky and most productive forms of information bartering: The translation from search results to list-building for the ultimate purpose of marketing to specific social networks.

Conversational Icebreakers – Breaking the Case Open

What are some key differences between query formation (interviewing computers) and interviewing people?

This question is best addressed from the vantage of the best post social media forum we have for using our investigations. This channel exists not just to do research, but to attract would-be peers, persons of interest, and even opportunities in the form of investors, partners, and hiring managers. That would be the now well-established act of self-publishing, through social media posts, blogging, and ebooks.

Blogging could be a cathartic way to unleash frustration. Nothing except self-restraint will keep us from posting or even over-sharing our pent-up furies. But with a little discipline, blogging can also be a way to build stature. A deliberative approach resists the role of the *wannabe authority*. Publishing as the Knowledge-ABLED investigator means (1) build bridges of understanding, and (2) cases for recommending courses of action through our research findings.

Every bridge built is a potential bartering situation that hinges on the familiar building blocks of social networking. If they seem familiar in an offline way, that's because they mirror the same engagement mix we'd expect to see when we're the targets: Think customer outreach in the toolbox of traditional marketing formulas, such as...

- Name dropping (testimonials)

- Expertise (FAQs)

- Dos and don'ts (checklists, red flags)

- Case studies (demonstrations)

- Product reviews (brokering producer-vendors)

- Customer surveys (brokering user-consumers)

So let's see how these approaches play to the strengths of Knowledge-ABLED bloggers like us.

Name Dropping (testimonials)

There's no shorter distance between two people than a second person connection. Getting from a third-party affiliation like a former company or location to a mutual acquaintance is a time-honored conversation starter. Well-connected blogs combine this *friend-of-a-friend* dynamic with an even more universal element for gaining market visibility and traction. That's the vanity of having one's name both mentioned and cemented to their own virtual outposts.

Look at any well-trodden blogging forum and we're likelier to take in news feed dynamics than static essays on our personal career choices. The only animals on Planet Blogosphere are the ones who check the indexes for their own appearances.

Expertise (FAQs)

"Frequently asked questions" or FAQs are a handy way to handhold the novices who are new to our sites and services. FAQs are an easy way to tell visitors not only what they need to understand as a layperson, but how they can get the most out of us, ideally as a client. That client perspective looms especially large here. FAQs are a necessary writing exercise for anyone who's ever had a hard time generalizing their special skills, or summarizing what they do.

FAQs are useful forums for accentuating our assets as service providers. But they're also a tool for initiating the relationship-building phase of potential allies and peers. Any recent task completed on a project worthy of repeating can be rephrased as an FAQ. Another opening ripe for FAQ fulfillment are lists such as dos and don'ts, and red flags. Again, they comport to any checklist that's generic enough for use as a general introduction to our skills and service offerings.

Case Studies (demonstrations)

There's no substitute for experience, but the runner-up is living vicariously through the episodic accounts of life in the trenches. In consulting circles and geeky-leaning market segments, these narratives stories are elevated as *success stories*. Such use cases confer status on both the narrator, her set of tools, and the larger team that completes a project. Hint: It helps build interest to introduce some well-plied narrative devices such as ingenuities inspired by scarcity, adversities. READ: Project team invents a novel approach while deploying it on a shoestring budget and unforgiving timeframe.

Ironically, the whole idea of success is such a subjective standard that any self-referential case study can ring false and self-serving. This perception prevails even when real and lasting value is delivered through the talents of these storytellers. Bloggers would do well to factor in community skepticism. This is the wariness groups develop when being pitched at the same moment they're comparing study results against their own requirements and experiences.

For that reason, focusing on what goes wrong speaks with greater directness and persuasion to our influence circles. War stories are the way to go here. They calibrate our BS detection settings. And if we're the survivors, we can speak with third-person objectivity, and first-person authenticity. Just because a fact-finding mission is about reaching a sensible decision, doesn't mean we only buy into level-headed rationales. I'm much likelier to believe a partisan who alternatively both loves and hates the product in question with the passion of a user, and producer ... AND implementer. War veterans bear the scars of their own misadventures. The cost of guessing wrong is an investment beyond the terms of any purchasing cycle or licensing deal. But an expert blog can shield readers from the same potential pitfalls, or even their own naivete.

Product Reviews (brokering producer-vendors)

One of the best ways to barter our direct experience with extended communities is to document our trials and errors with the tools of our trades. It's perennial marketing gospel that motivated customers are likelier to buy from direct recommendations (word-of-mouth) than from the indirect suggestions of promotional media (advertising). Blogging represents a wider, more persistent opportunity, short of sharing a first-person affiliation with an active user of the service/product under consideration. Blogging provides a total third-person stranger (us), with no direct stake in their decisions, other than to be cited as a trusted adviser in future buying cycles.

Consummate experts can leverage their independent authority status as brokers for would-be customers in the evaluation stages of their pending purchases. That role of influencer can be expanded to include both product vendors and service providers as well, depending in no small part on the level of traffic directed to the reviews we post.

Customer Surveys (brokering user-consumers)

One of the benefits of any sound diagnostic is not only to identify what customers want, but their perceptions (what they think they want). The Biggest Picture is a credible way to add context and volume to weigh the specific features or assets our clients offer against the demands of the marketplace. Tapping into those preferences is doubly desirable when those requests can be satisfied today. It's not on the drawing board for a next release. It's a tool ready for the using, and a finding ready for acting on.

A TBP approach is especially useful as a substitute for close-ended questions normally found in marketing surveys. Typically, perceptions are searchable when the content producer is not limited by a set of predefined choices, or multiple choice responses. The respondent is free to communicate in an open-ended way that may or may not match any of the pre-canned responses.

THE PULSE-TAKING VIRTUES OF RESEARCH BLOGS

Demonstrating our research acumen is another essential ingredient of building a following as researcher-bloggers.

One way to use social media tools, deviating from the personal updates, is to substitute topic-based events of greater consequence. RSS is the streaming tool for tuning us into the disjointed and often inane details of those slipping in and out of real-time texting consciousness. But the same medium can track unfolding events of interest to us and our communities while *keeping the lights on,* even if we skip a cycle in our own updates or publishing schedules.

One thing to remember is that blog posts are rarely read out loud – let alone discussed in public. It is the internal workings of one's ruminations given the posterity of our life's recordings. Our every move captured between <send> commands has the potential to gain the affirmations or disapprovals of people with whom we share no other histories. In the following excerpt, the author, Vicki Abelson writes of the cascading effect of a checkbox change to the marriage status panel on her Facebook Page:

> *"I took to snooping to see what he was up to. He was 'interested' in women. And men. But, women, first. I never quite got over that. I don't think he meant anything by it, but it seemed a disrespect. At least I perceived it that way. In response, I removed 'Married' from my info (because I'm mature that way), not realizing that it would post on all of my friends' news feeds. I was instantly deluged with, 'What happened?' Little did they, or I, know at the time – a lot. I reposted 'Married' later that day, but it never meant quite the same thing again.* **(Abelson, 2011)**[10]

The real tease in this passage is the notion that the simple transacting of a change to a digitized form could spiral into such a defining moment in the estrangement of two people. That simple signal change did the job that first launched a force much bigger than the news business. That would be the syndication industry. But we no longer need to rely on the kindness of press agents. We've hatched a whole new reward system for passing messages with RSS.

Good news for us knowledge-ENABLED news aggregators. It's a system dependent on our query formation skills. What it's not is beholden to information providers!

Dynamic Blogging

One of the merits of blogging is that we need to solder the pipes once. The plumbing should work fine after that, whether we have something new to post or not. The tools themselves will pull the content in based on the news feeds we stream. Unlike working on our desktop, we don't have to create new material, update our interests, or be on-the-hook for every new development in our fields.

Dynamic blogging refers to the hands-off approach of piecing together updates to time-sensitive topics that appeal to our site visitors. It's hands-off because a successful RSS query practically feeds itself without our intervention. If this concept sounds familiar, think back to the event triggers that resonated in The Biggest Picture groupings we framed for the corporate and marketing functions within Taco Bell. These triggers can be pulled for designing RSS queries too. Here is a sampling of action-based queries with an emphasis on the semantics used to anticipate these finely-tuned news feeds:

FIGURE 5.15: Sample Event Triggers in Criminal and Civic Crimes for Content Aggregation

Criminal Cases	Civil Cases
"missing (child OR teens OR children OR person) (police OR manslaughter OR murder OR homicide OR suspected)"	"(misled OR misleading OR misinform OR misinformed) (customers OR clients OR shareholders OR employees)"
"missing (neighbors OR loved OR family OR persons) OR disappearance (family OR loved) -war –disaster	"(overstated OR overstate OR overstating) (revenue OR earnings OR revenues OR income)"
"police (raids OR raid)"	"(punitive OR disciplinary) (actions OR action)" (corporate OR company OR business OR industry)
"street gang" OR "street gangs" OR "gang (shooting OR violence OR warfare)"	"(siphoned OR siphon OR rip OR ripped) off"
("organized crime" OR mafia OR mobster OR mobsters)" OR "crime (bosses OR boss)"	"(windfall OR excessive) (sales OR profit OR profits OR margins)" OR profiteering OR profiteers OR "price gouging"
(allegations OR accused) "(sex OR sexual) (crime OR assault OR harassment)" -military -defense –sports	"collar (prison OR prisons OR crime OR crimes)" OR "executives * (incarceration OR incarcerated)" OR "minimum security"

On the Job Blogging

The guarantee of lifetime employment vaporized in the recession of the early 1990s. **(Pozen, 2012)**[11] Since then, the economic reality of the great foreseeable future is that most of us need to diversify our income sources, regardless of our job titles, client rosters, salary histories, or earning potential. There is no corporate belt-slackening that awaits the next post recession rebound. For professionals dependent on salary income, continuous improvement is not an option.

The precarious state of the economy on job security is a kick in the pants for all of us. One response is to use our blogging mediums to raise our research games in meeting these professional challenges.

FIGURE 5.16: Research Blog in Support of Investigative Practice and Research Services

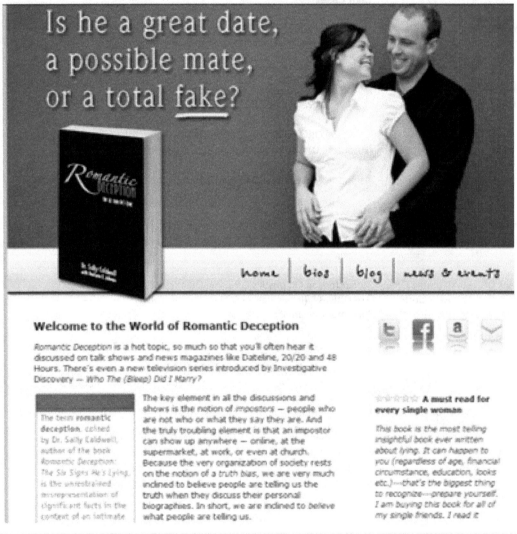

Here, former student and author Darlene Adams profiles her seminal work on patterns of betrayal in romantic deception. It's an expertise she continues to ply through her blogging topics.[12]

It's no secret that a shaky economy is unspoken code for going back to school to bump-up in credentials and upgrade job skills. There is no unconfirmed rumor leaking here that social networking sites now define the crossroads for matching client and job leads to project requirements and hiring managers. Another fertile opportunity open to the Knowledge-ABLED is the research blog as a showcase for our investigations: Be it as a job applicant, business consultant, or ranking expert in our fields of interest.

Using Blogs as a Research Medium

For much of this book, we've taken a dim and even elitist view towards web-based marketing. The abstraction of increased understanding takes a backseat to the concrete goal of generating sales. Most of this book has been polemical in nature. That means writing not only a how-to book but why becoming Knowledge-ABLED is an essential 21st Century skill, regardless of our vocational directions and career choices.

Searching Out Loud: Giving Voice to Independent Investigations | Marc Solomon

Okay. So being a skillful researcher has two immediate paybacks:

> 1. We can background check our future employers and clients like it's nobody's business.

> 2. We can showcase those skills as educators and consultants for hire.

Do you detect a subtle shift here? We're moving our background checks into the foreground. We're not just practicing our craft, but communicating it to a potential audience. These recipients are our peers. Hopefully, they get both our blogs and the fact they can benefit directly from collaborations with us.

One thing prefaced in final course assignments with my student investigators was dedicated to blogging goals and objectives. I prefaced the final project with these two questions for them as aspiring PIs:

> 1. How can you break into a new profession?

And if you are an established professional...

> 2. How do you hone your act, or create a new niche to your best advantage?

To my students, a PI-related blog was their calling card for hooking up with other PIs on the cases they tracked, the skills they cultivated, and, the job opportunities likelier to arise from networking than from scanning job sites or company websites.

FIGURE 5.17: Research Blog Transformed from Victims' Rights Examples to a Cross-cultural Exchange between Communities

Above, a former student identifies some of the common misconceptions about legal protections and loopholes and enriches the forum with a CSE ("custom search engine") that captures topical feeds in her native dialect.

These breakthroughs were once attained by playing *the media card*. That means writing a freelance article for a trade periodical. Here the writing project is the excuse for beginning a dialog with a subject expert or potential colleague. We put ourselves out there. They accept our invitations for an interview.

Blogs however, are not necessarily about interviewing experts. They can be linked to those search targets. Those links are especially germane when picking topics to write about where we share a mutual interest with the leaders in our fields. So blogs are good for attracting the attention of the folks we need to meet. In my case, they were also useful for giving my virtual learners a meaningful grade for participation in my courses!

That demonstration included how well they integrate some of the lessons we've already completed into the making of our blogs. For instance, the social bookmarking tool we're now acquainted with for capturing useful websites was repurposed as a blog-based content source. Their choice of topic was also important – not so much *what* subject they chose but how well their blog page connects with the topicality of their subject expertise. Finally, their ability to reflect on these developments in their postings was the single most unique way to make their own contribution. Singling out opinions about news, commentary, and the evidence used to support them.

THE CATHARTIC BLOGGER

Recent behavioral studies suggest that blogging has emotional benefits for bloggers. Micro-blogging on Twitter with its 140 character limit is even more of a rush. Dispense with the laws of rhetoric, and all that's left is us trusting our guts.

Don't think you're being heard about a particular grievance? Pontificate freely. In cyberspace, no one's going to curtail the right to rant (whether anyone hears your rant or not).[13] Need to share some inspiration or shed some light? Go for it. These positive impacts are similar to more traditional forms of record-keeping like a diary. Only the Internet transforms a personal medium into a social one. Every keystroke is recorded and shared within a self-selecting audience.

It's the size of that audience that inspires the commercial voice of blogging: Here's how to attract visitors and harvest their emails, here's how to become a megaphone in the blogosphere, here's how to increase your income by allowing advertisers on your site, etc. Sound familiar? Maybe you're old enough to remember the snake oil salesmen who bid up the price of internet domain names?

Our non-merchandising motivations for blogging are twofold:

1. The community aspects of blogging enables us to extend our relationships from our immediate circle to a virtual one (and if we're lucky a virtuous one as well). This is a group of peers limited only by a common language and a common interest. Done right, it is that community that will expand to suggest new career horizons, maybe even our own career paths.

2. It is the calling card aspect of blogs that enables the would-be contacts we've come to know through our own research. Research blogs enables the people we approach to get up-to-speed on (1) mutual interests, (2) common goals, (3) professional contacts, and (4) uniquely held opinions, priorities, and forms of expressing them.

That's our primary reason for using our blogs as platforms for staging our Knowledge-ABLED assets. It's not to rise in the ranking formulas, but first to find our own voice in the research we do, and second, to have the work speak for itself.

<u>**Picking a Blogging Theme**</u>

As an investigator, we typically use blogs to cover a particular *beat* or interest that attracts or keeps us in our selected profession. Maybe it's an issue actually related to the digital world such as fraud detection and identity theft. Maybe it's a round-up of specific crime-fighting resources that the public can use to solve crimes, address legal problems, or petition on their own behalf. Maybe it's a pursuit of the details about local crimes and tracking them to trial. Maybe it's about the virtual presence of other investigators, and how they market themselves to the very communities you know or aspire to join?

Blogging themes are only limited by your imagination: Summoning a common experience worth sharing inside a virtual community. For our purposes, *the what* of our research blog addresses the types of reporting methods you'll enlist on your site. There are three common approaches and you are not limited to picking only one. In fact, a hybrid of several methods might improve our calling card status as a research blogger:

1. **Opinion-editorial:** This is the most common and popular approach to blogging. The blog becomes a *soap box* or launch pad for our take on recent noteworthy events. Op-ed blogs are especially prevalent in the political arena. From our perspective, your own political affiliation is not important. What is critical is that we cite other published sources that both inspire and support our passions and skepticisms. Supporting evidence and research methods should be out in front. This is our contribution to shaping current debates, dialogs, and inevitably the laws and policies we aspire to influence.

2. **Events and developments:** This is the correct card to play once we're comfortable with the kibitzing and bartering that happens between members of the same or related communities. First is the quiver in the bow of all barterers: Knowing how and where to anticipate the unexpected before it becomes breaking news. The second step is to set information traps loose on your blogging site. Tools such as RSS feeds and email alerts are especially helpful for building event listings based on topics, locations, and institutional calendars, i.e. legislation or legal proceedings. In **Unit Six**, we'll try our hand at **Information Trapping**, and the role of RSS feed readers as one way to tease out details lost in ad hoc site-by-site capture.

3. **Summaries and tools:** Summaries take a page from op-ed and event-based blogs to round-up sites and pages that serve specific professional circles. The goal of a summary provider is less to assess the quality of each resource, and more to classify these links in a useful way for our site visitors. Another tool we introduced in **Unit Two** are customized search engines ("CSEs"). Building our own CSE enables blog visitors to classify the content they find according to the search groupings we configure.

BLOGS AS CALLING CARDS

As I've tried to suggest in these bartering arrangements, blogs are not just excuses to vent or glad-hand the folks we're hoping will return our calls.

Blogs are a showcase for experience. A resume is static and self-contained. A media kit or backgrounder on your services and references is out-of-date the moment it's ink or paper. A blog is dynamic. The deeper our involvement, the more dynamic it becomes, and, the likelier we'll attract others to it by connecting...

- What's happening on the web related to our professional goals and personal interests, and

- The extended community of peers we're trying to reach, build, or augment.

The research blog can tap into digital news, opinion and media (videos, podcasts, slide presentations, etc.) that concern us. But how do we get from a casual to an ardent interest? How do we go from an occasional way of becoming informed, to a systematic capturing of the subject domain we're trying to master?

Does it means attending webcasts, subscribing to journals, and getting updates to every last word on our field of interest? If the answer is yes, I promise you two things: you will fail, and you will lose interest before that sense of failure takes hold.

That doesn't mean we need to throw cold water on our investigations every time we miss a blogging cycle:

1. What if we could be exhaustive in our research without suffering mental exhaustion in the process?

2. What if we didn't need to check every conceivable source, and could still account for each one?

3. What if we could filter what each source was saying, spared the distraction of redundant and irrelevant information?

4. What if we could tweak our query refinements so that only importance passes through them?

PULLING SELECTIVE CONTENT TOWARDS US THROUGH RSS

You wouldn't need to spend extra time and resources to transition from blogger to researcher. But you would need two points of information:

1. What are RSS feeds, and

2. How do I put them to work?

RSS is the way any web-based publisher can package and send updates about the content they publish: Be it news site, marketing campaign, or blog post. Also RSS is flexible. It's not just a conduit for articles. Yes it includes traditional content we might have subscribed to in the offline world of newspapers and magazines. But much of what's carried never existed in print form. Episodes from broadcast media programs, education-based tutorials, and entertainment-based outlets from film, the performing arts, and popular sports are all fair game for RSS feeds.[14]

Do you review your email or familiar sources with a weary feeling that the meaning behind what you're reading can be measured in fractions instead of volumes?

I know what you're thinking: I can barely keep up with my email. How can I possibly open another towering in-box of messages demanding my attention? I thought you said RSS would mean spending less time on screens!

I did. But you need to define your content turf. You also need a good set of controls for tuning the kinds of feeds you get back, let alone the kind you too would find worthy of publishing in your blog. That tool is called a feed reader and we'll get to those.

Our event triggers in the form of news feeds, our commentary, and our social circles now travel in a style that research bloggers are accustomed to. And it's called RSS.

But first here's something else to know about RSS. It's not just about pushing more content than we can handle in our face. Yes, it will do that if we let it. But we can also use RSS as a pull mechanism. *Pull* means that we've already screened a selective chunk of material and we've decided to share it with our site visitors. RSS enables us to see not only oceans of content but the gold nuggets worthy of interaction.

Let me explain.

FIGURE 5.18: Research Blogs Worthy of Subscribing

BRB's Public Records Blog
syndicated content powered by FeedBurner

FeedBurner makes it easy to receive content updates in My Yahoo!, Newsgator, Bloglines, and other news readers.

Learn more about syndication and FeedBurner...

A message from this feed's publisher:

Subscribe Now!

...with web-based news readers. Click your choice below:

MY YAHOO!

feedly   netvibes

SubToMe)

...with other readers:

(Choose Your Reader)

Current Feed Content

Decentralization of Small Claims In CT
Posted:2017-10-03 13:53:00 UTC-05:00

Effective Monday, October 16, 2017, the Centralized Small Claims Office located at **80 Washington Street, Hartford, CT 06106** will be closed. Any new small claims cases filed on or after Friday, September 1, 2017, either paper or electronically, will have an answer date after October 16, 2017, and will be transferred to the small claims docket at the appropriate judicial district or housing session location.

Judge Rules that Colorado' Sex Offender Registry Law is Unconstitutional
Posted:2017-10-03 13:50:46 UTC-05:00

On August 31, 2017, the U.S. District Court in Colorado ruled that Colorado's sex offender registry law is cruel and unusual punishment. Per U.S. District Court Judge Richard Matsch's ruling, the Colorado's sex-offender registry violated the Constitutional rights of three sex offenders who sued regarding the way the public has access to the list.

Per the ruling, Judge Matsch found that Colorado's registration act poses a "serious threat of retaliation, violence, ostracism, shaming, and other unfair and irrational treatment from the public" for sex offenders and their families.

All blogs are subscribable (just like news feeds on all social media sites). Whether they're worth tracking relates to their thoroughness and the dynamic nature of the turf they cover. In this case the BRB news feed is tracking the complex and fluid nature of public records access on a state-by-state basis.

One common use of RSS feeds is to stream or pull the sites we flag in a social bookmarking tool like Reddit out to our blogging site. Another tool called a news aggregator enables us to submit articles we find important, endorse the submissions of others, and comment on the news items we flag with our own unique perspective.

Another benefit of a decent RSS reader is to flag items. While it's helpful to assign stories to our reading pile, there's an added benefit for bloggers. The main reason for the clips is to handpick specific stories that we'll want to showcase in reposting to our own sites. This feature enables us to be both filters, and amplifiers for our own readership.

The Complementary Nature of Blogs and RSS

We're coming to the end of our presentation cycle. But the main agenda item here is not blogging, actually. It's about the symbiotic relationship between blogs and RSS ("Really Simple Syndication"). In addition to social bookmaking and blogging, this business of RSS feeds (Feed Demon) will be helpful to us in a number of ways.

Query formation is designed to produce *aboutness*. Aboutness implies that our search results actually address the issue that inspired the search. RSS is aboutness plus timeliness. It's what's going on in our field which is not just topic-related but you-specific – READ: Your own niche. *Niche* here covers your blog as personal branding statement, and how others will come to know you. This is number one Google hit, with a bullet now.

RSS is for people who don't like to search. Instead of formulating new queries every time out, think about this: The liberation of creating the definitive tweak and have new dividends arrive each day that reaffirm this pay-off. That's what happens when our searches product 70% or better aboutness. The context is true to our intentions. We want to connect that confidence to one specific location. Where the only information that's allowed in is the result of our own discriminating filters.

We've caught lightning in a bottle. But in the case of RSS it can strike often, depending on how exacting or specific we are about what we're trying to catch.

FIGURE 5.19: Research Blog as a Subscribable News Feed

We've just hit the subscribe button. Here's what an XML script looks rendered as an HTML page in a browser. News readers are tools for assimilating news feeds into searchable and categorical archive.

Along those lines, the RSS reader is really *our pond.* That's where we're likeliest to run into the kind of developments that not only grab our attention but implore us to take action. Once we can establish a meaningful stream of news, site updates, and trackable events, it follows that we plan calls, emails, webcasts, and social calendars around the rhythms of the RSS reader.

So how do we capture lightning in a bottle?

It might make sense to come up with RSS sources related to our investigations. As we'll see in **Unit Six**, one painless way to do this is to...

- Click on the [File] dropdown in an RSS Reader called FeedDemon.

- Select 'Find New Feeds.'

I put in the phrase "public records" and got back some spot-on reports, directories, and trackers about what law and licensing records are coming online as well as some neat CSI ("crime scene investigation") mapping tools vis-a-vis Google Maps.

One other no-brainer is to seek out others that we want to reciprocate fellow bloggers, either by commenting on their posts, and/or including them in our blogrolls.

Blogrolls

Another benefit of a news aggregation site pertains to another RSS mainstay called a blogroll. Blogrolls are links to your favorite bloggers that can travels dynamically to our research blogs via RSS. Blogrolls are an especially good way to create a community presence, and the sense of respect, comity, and peer review suggested by these assemblies. Another benefit of blogrolls is that no two bloggers have the same take on the same subject (Twitter bots withstanding).

One blogger may be focused on case law involving child abductions. Another might be tracking law enforcement efforts to coordinate efforts around state boundaries. Yet a third may be looking at the reporting of Amber Alerts, along with their completeness, accuracy, and effectiveness of databases listing these abductions and their status.

From a topical perspective, blogrolls represent a cross-section of domains that all share a mutual goal or common interest. What lies at the center of that interest? That's where our blog needs to be...

- In the topics we address

- The sources we draw from

- The views we espouse, and most importantly

- The expertise we're cultivating

Another use of RSS is to generate customized search results that signify a string of significant developments that address our blogging topics. Here's where we Knowledge-ENABLE those assets we've assembled in units past through our...

- Understanding of query formation through syntax and semantics,

- Expectations around sources through oceans, lakes and ponds, and

- Motivations ascribed to sources through the **Provider Conjugation Framework**.

Each of the models can be instructive for site visitors – particularly for our more engaged peers. Those user-producers we introduced earlier in this section.

Works in-progress

Let's say for instance if you want to display a feed of reported Amber Alerts by region. A series of Google queries uses a mixture of syntax and semantics such as [local:Massachusetts] and the following search statement:

> **"(issue OR issues OR issued OR issuing) * amber alert"**

The asterisk is the placeholder for any number of possible terms that can appear between the predicate, and the objective phrase here, our targeting of Amber Alerts.[15]

We can reject Google's definitions around news providers if we want to apply some basic OLP ("Oceans, Lakes and Ponds") principles. Instead, we can create a CSE with our own Google account that's based on our own sets of information providers.

One grouping could be local university pages where we're interested in tracking job openings or courses being offered in our interest area. Another could be local media sources where we're tracking the coverage of a highly-charged murder investigation. Still another? A series of highly influential blogs, all attempting to influence the outcome of an ongoing dispute, policy, or looming election.

That last example begs an important question: How does one determine the popularity of a particular blogger? It's hard to know who to pay attention to with the barrier to entry so low, and breadth of blogging topics. Reddit communities, Twitterers, and Facebook manifestos all compete for attention by posting the stories they find, commenting on them, voting for other posts, and forming networks in the process. That's the dynamic at work in news aggregation sites. That's where the popularity of our search results are driven by the dedication of a core group of daily participants, the first-person power users.

How do we find them?

There's no shortage of algorithms all chasing the golden fleece of social media supremacy. An ideal tool would integrate...

- Usage, including other stories they've submitted along with their comments
- That slippery, defining metric called 'authority' based in part on the number of links to a particular blog site from other referring winks, prods, and actual commentary
- Instances where our work has been cited by other bookmarking sites, news communities, personal pages, and tweets?

That's always a plus, right?

What does this say about our own blogging efforts?

Should we invest every idle moment in becoming a disciple of the viral marketing bug? The fervor that resides in social media junkies in order to place their discoveries in some select tier of elite influencers?

That's for you to decide.

But aside from questions of status, influence, and reputation, it certainly helps to familiarize ourselves with the tools and practices needed pull up X chair at Y table. That's no arranged seating plan. That's us developing a grasp, a voice, and eventual discussions with potential allies and colleagues through the virtual presence of the blogosphere.

Custom Search for Blogging

As we just intimated, another way to point your engine in the direction of the right collection is to determine that ourselves. Specialty or custom search enables us to literally perform a search within a search. Here the engine can trap useful sites by limiting the search to specific site domains or URL terms.

The CSE accentuates our skills as content curators, as well as query formation developers. We can introduce entirely different angles to a news feed based on the conventions followed in these different publishing traditions. Case-in-point: Looking for name droppings due to promotions and announcements? Then the script favors the targeted job titles of appointed executives in the industries we're tracking.[16]

Wire Services

- upi.com/*
- reuters.com/*
- ap.org/*
- businesswire.com/*
- prnewswire.com/*

If we're partial to more assessment-minded and analytical fare, then we want to separate pull media from push. This is the kind of information that we used to pay for. Occasionally we still do. That means focusing on major business media sources:

Major Business Media

- inc.com/*
- fastcompany.com/*
- economist.com/*
- businessweek.com/*
- forbes.com/*
- ft.com/*

We can always encircle those old standby networks in the antiquated world of broadcasting. Here we cast our horizons on a national level to see how widely spread an awareness is our search targets:

Broadcast Media

- cnbc.com/*

- abcnews.go.com/*

- cbsnews.com/*

- msnbc.com/*

- bbc.co.uk/*

- npr.org/*

If we seek a more local flavoring, our event triggers will accentuate those functions through the regional business press and the business section of local metro dailies. Think local when considering regional business community, lobbying efforts, business permits, seed funding, and connections to related academic and non-profits:

Newspapers

- latimes.com/*

- nytimes.com/*

- washingtonpost.com/*

- chicagotribune.com/*

- wsj.com/*

- Crains[*changes by edition for given locality*].com/*

The overriding point here isn't that media groupings have their own rhythms in the form of their turfs, news selection priorities, editorial leanings, and presentation styles. It's that tools like RSS and custom search engines enable the news junkies in us to be both discriminating curators, bloggers, brokers, and yes, investigators.

SECTION 5:3 | Message Delivery–

The Presenter as Exhibit

We've accumulated lots of information heading into that client presentation, final dissertation, or job interview. Our local drive, note-taking apps, and Google Docs are jammed with search log tracking of queries, results, and sources to evidence patterns. They contain what we've investigated, how we've done so, and hopefully, a range of outcomes about where it all leads.

This information is in the form of opinion, data, and perhaps additional people to interview, actions to take, or mysteries that will go unsolved. These findings will be presented to the client along with recommendations in the final report.

We've finally come to the final research frontier. No, it's not unmasking the wizard behind the smoke and mirrors. It's showing our cards. It's placing the unvarnished truth on the meeting table so that our associates, students, supervisors, clients, and community peers can decide for themselves:

1. Do they see how we traveled from our original premise to our final conclusion?

2. Do they buy it?

3. Do they see a personal upside for following through on our recommendations? How about for increasing their own commitments?

4. Are there overlapping interests here – can they be unified in pursuit of a common goal?

It all boils down to this: How our research informs and influences their thinking, behavior, and ultimately their actions. How do we close that distance between *our* words, and *their* actions?

In this section we stop weighing the evidence. We start weighing in on the facts, opinions, and supporting details worth evidencing. We begin with the selection process: Which facts? Whose opinions? What order? When to conclude? Where to end up?

CONFIRMABLE FACTS, EDUCATED GUESSES

Confirmable facts and educated guesses result when we apply the three levels of **Quality Control**, which allow us to...

- Offer our best *guesstimate*
- Base our hunches on hard evidence
- Resolve competing claims colored by perception and/or self-interest and self-preservation

What do we learn in our interviews and research that we can incorporate into our final client presentation? Are there staggering revelations that linger on well past the point of discovery, of self-evident explanation?

Is it a dead match between our original expectations and our final conclusions? It usually helps to put away the iPhones and Androids when we count in the *surprise factor:* How much the outcome deviates from the core thesis or assumptions made at the beginning of the project.

The greater the surprise, the closer to the front of our report that surprise should be placed.

Then there are results that are neither dutiful confirmations, nor shocking revelations. But they still warrant the *front page* treatment. Maybe our findings are not unexpected. Could be this is just yesterday's news to the client. Perhaps our conclusions will have a familiar ring.

But what if we propose a big departure from business-as-usual? What if it has an unfamiliar ring, or even a disruptive one? We might become implicated in our own investigations when we go poking our sniffers into unsuspecting places. Here our research credibility may take a hit. One case-in-point: Our research pops open the trial balloon our client was floating about a potential business partner, maybe even a suitor of their C-suite?

Here are a few sounding bells to consider:

> 1. Do we shift the emphasis away from the big pay-off of a long-shot opportunity, and revisit the original premise?
>
> 2. Do we plant some alternatives that deviate from our initial assertions?
>
> 3. Do we expand the investigation to include competing theories and explanations?

When Judgment Calls

These are judgment calls. They rely as much on our skills of correctly reading client hopes and aspirations as drawing out any specific finding or conclusion. Are we confirming what they believed before our search project? Are we delivering on their prior expectations – or dashing them? The only way to know for sure is to trace the mission to its source. That means we already know our client's motivation. We knew the *why* before we got to work on the research.

Motive is not a given. It's the exception when intentions *don't* leave us in the dark. Our clients don't want to give us any preconceptions about what we'll find. They don't want to confuse our fresh perspectives with their own hardened biases or presumptions. They might not want us to know their motives because they would feel compromised. Most core motivations stick close to home.

Most reasons that drive an investment in research are self-serving ones, revealing more about selfish impulses than about the bigger picture of who else wins or loses from the impact of the answer. Regardless of the question, that's the card the Knowledge-ABLED are left holding.

The Powerlessness of Numbers

Then there are groups. There's another distinct possibility why we're kept in the dark if we're presenting to a board, panel, or committee. The person contacting us to do the work doesn't know either. They are a funnel between the original question-poser and us. Theirs is not to question why but often to shield the identity of their superiors. Trying for motive, seeking priorities, or even clarifying objectives can be at best a waste of our time, or worse, a fight we did not intend to pick. Challenging a funnel to be more forthcoming is a fight the researcher does not win.

So getting to motive can be unflattering to our client. It can be frustrating to deal with surrogates like funnels who know little beyond protecting their bosses. What's the reward for us as the researcher?

The number one question for any investigator has little to do with social networks, access to resources, or even topflight interview skills. It's not about asking informed questions – unless they lead to a determination of what the answer is worth. That is the researcher's motivation. And by *worth,* I don't mean self-worth, or even a more social context like worthy or commendable. I mean literally the commercial price that the client has factored into the calculation they made before calling on us.

Here is the basic reduction of the *worth equation*:

> **Worth = outcome + fee**

Say for instance that casting doubt on your client's connection to a criminal action has this upside: The potential to save them both criminal penalties and some potentially hefty fees in mounting their legal defense.

What the answer's worth to a client will not only help you set a fee, but inform the extent you're willing to go. Equally helpful, motive can tell you where you will go astray looking for superfluous information that costs time, materials, and conceivably your reputation as an investigator.

Knowing why is not a failure-proof formula. It doesn't always translate the answers we give into dollars and per diems. For instance, let's say our client is a restaurant owner. She's reasonably certain she is being ripped off by her employees. But she has no clue just how widespread the problem is. Does that mean the burden of education falls to us? Does that mean we need to first investigate the numbers to measure the risks for a business of her nature and size? That may be a risk worth *our* taking.

As we educate our client, we're also informing ourselves. It's earnings from learnings. Not only are we learning about what we're helping to prove, prevent, debunk, or confirm. Most importantly, we're here to help recoup the payback for our clients' investment in our investigative services.

Decision-making Traps

> *"Beliefs without decisions are just sterile."*
>
> **– Nassim Nicholas Taleb, the Black Swan**

We talked earlier of the necessity for action in our delivery of search results and client recommendations. We also spoke of the need to understand client motivation which informs...

- How we present our findings,
- How we maintain distance from our investigations, and
- Even how much we bill for them.

But it's not just positive strokes or clear actions we're out to communicate with our findings. In fact, our quest for the former can undermine our status as researchers. It's the oldest sellout in the annals of consulting. Yes, our own self-interest can easily compromise the validity of the research.

Who knew!

Pre-drawn conclusions and overlooked assumptions are the telltale signs of undue diligence and flawed rationales. But those warning bells ring across the presentation table as well. In fact, it's easy to dismiss research that doesn't account for ulterior motives: What our audience hopes to gain from our labors. **(Morville, 2005)**[17]

The term 'professional researcher' is about as exploratory as the range of topics and outcomes we are collectively called on to investigate. But one universal dictum is that commercial gain and self-interest do not compromise our investigations. Can different researchers come to different conclusions from the same body of evidence?

Heck, yeah.

If anything, we can be less skeptical around competing explanations than those drawn from a single, uniform, unquestioning point-of-view.

Methodologies as Quality Checks

However, this healthy diversity of opinion does not hold in the evidence-gathering of the research. Opinion surveys are believed when there are fewer opinions about how that survey was conducted. The methodologies we use to draw our samples and test hypotheses should be transparent. They should bear repeating, just like the air pressure in our tires, or the blood pressure in our veins.

A gauge is not a reliable measurement tool if it is based on intuition and individual preference. So too, with the research we present. There must be no doubt that the same search stands up to repeated observation by similarly skilled and resourced professionals.

In real life, we do not care about simple, raw probability. We worry about the consequences. We fret over the magnitude of an event once it occurs. As Nassim Taleb points out in his polemic *the Black Swan,* our clients need to move beyond the mitigating muddle of true/false into if/then: What are the probabilities for understanding each possibility we consider as...

- The consequence of the true
- The severity of the false **(Taleb, 2007)**[18]

The Nerves We Fray

This larger dimension of usefulness takes on a whole new life, when we consider what our clients and peers, will do with our investigations. Our case might be winding down, but their sleeves may first be rolling up. In fact, now that they've heard from us, the very notion of how close or far the client is from their ultimate goal may shift as well.

We may never know the loops we're closing or the mysteries we're exposing. We may well remain in the dark once the projector light dims. We may surrender our badges to building security, no closer to understanding what we've done to...

- Shape our clients' perspectives,
- Weigh their priorities,
- Confirm their intuitions and biases, and
- Trigger their initiatives.

But the investigation itself is not compromised just because our research is transparent and our clients' end game is opaque. Keeping their cards hidden doesn't absolve our need to anticipate how these implications can play out. We can't insist on correct interpretations. We can't *impose* a set of recommendations. But we need to step through the minefields with the understanding we may not step deftly over every improvised explosive.

Can we reel in the very same forces we're about to unleash? This is an off-stage question best raised before the final presentation is even scheduled. Here are three examples of dialing back on the buttons we're about to push, and nerves we may well fray:

1. **Raising Doubts** – Be careful not to confuse unexpected survey results with hypothetical scenarios. This broader perspective can come uncomfortably close to a client's traditional allies and partners. *Spooking* our clients can overshadow our informing them. Present a doomsday scenario that falls outside the sponsor's imagination, and we risk dooming the presentation too.

2. **Idle Speculations** – Don't engage in presenting simple true or false guessing games. Leave the logical problems to the theoreticians. A Knowledge-ABLED investigation is about getting our presentation audience off the dime. Not detachable speculation and abstraction, but informed commitment and action.

3. **Shock Factors** – Know our client's expectations coming into the presentation. The greater the surprises we come to share, the greater the distance the audience needs to travel to grasp, let alone digest, buy into, or follow-up on the assertions we're making.

Losing Our Sway

No piece of client intelligence is more important than cycling through what the client tells themselves without prompting. The revelation clients are hoping to learn isn't new to their thinking. It's to confirm what they want to believe:

"See? I told you so!"

That's the reflexive posturing known as confirmation bias. If the evidence supports it, then our client was right at first sight: The empress sees herself in the mirror – and a dazzling outfit on has she! **(O'Toole, Bennis, 2009)**[19]

If case evidence refutes confirmation bias, what does this portend for us? What happens if we refuse to dress or redress this naked truth? Do we paint the *yes men* as suitors, seeking favor as informants? Are they selectively providing only counsel that supports our clients' deeply held convictions? How strong a hold? Strong enough to reinforce their own frame of reference – that much is clear.

<u>**Uninvited Guests**</u>

Not all stakeholders gathered around our presentation table are invited guests. In fact, a few of them don't even have Facebook pages. There manage to sneak in regardless of how well we prepare. So don't be surprised. But do sit up and pay attention when the following meeting crashers slip through the conference door:

1. **Anchoring** – Our minds are more welcoming when we come to an issue fresh. Once an initial impression is formed, it's harder to maintain a detached perspective. Sometimes we're joining in momentarily. Other times, we're jumping in with both feet. We expect *a return.* We've invested, sometimes, without consciously knowing it.

2. **Memorability** – We are unduly influenced by the tyranny of immediacy. We must instantly stop what we're doing. Here's the newest blip that some messenger slipped under the door where we hung that Do-Not-Disturb sign. No consequence is too mundane. There is no history or future.There is only the presumption of the most pressing issues at the moment.

3. **Status Quo** – Figureheads and institutional managers tend to let decisions languish, preferring incremental changes to sweeping transformations. This is especially true of institutions that pay with their mistakes through their exposure to risk. That potential far outweighs any potential gains from shaking things up. Risk aversion is often masked by an aggressive research effort: We look for reasons to do nothing.

4. **Sunk Cost** – How well do we know our presentation guests can certainly influence how much we disclose what we know *of them*? The more removed we are from their networks, the more clearly we can objectify them. We see them as part of a crowd, a breed, tribe, or trend. But that detachment makes a stakeholder more reluctant to move beyond the past and steer clear of lingering questions, competing explanations, and conflicting evidence. As we saw in first party PCF, decision-makers remain vested in their past decisions.

5. **Biology** – Psychologist and author Daniel Kahneman connects the weight our bodily needs place on our critical judgment. Nature calls in more varied and subtle ways than our non-presenting selves might stop and consider: Low blood sugar, for one thing. Kahneman points to the increased leniency among Israeli parole judges after a lunch break. Just before snack time? Not the optimal time to have one's case reviewed. **(Speed of Thought, 2011[20])** Before we connect the dots for our clients, let's draw one between direct causes and their effects: In this case, the lowering of glucose levels and admission of these uninvited guests at our meetings.

PROGNOSTICATIONS

The annals of record-keeping are more about keeping history, than making it or predicting its course. More than researchers, fact checkers, and evidence-gatherers, our clients harbor a not-so-secretive desire. They wish that we were bona fide time travelers. Our time travel credentials can remove all doubts and apply all-certain approvals. We are fortune tellers disguised as investigators. This delusion needs to be understood and appreciated from the clients' perspective. A bias towards closing loops, and completing them within one's incomplete experience is what Taleb concludes in the Black Swan:

> *"We are too narrow-minded a species to consider the possibility of events straying from our mental projections."* **(Taleb, 2007)**[21]

It is not our job to be soothsayers. But that's what we do every time we're asked to place a bet, or handicap the probabilities of what we'll encounter down the road. The one thing that we can do as researchers is take the client outside their own self-referential views of the world. We can increase their appreciation for the great number of unknowns.

Still, who wants to be shown their own insignificance in the wider scheme of things? Wouldn't hard knocks afford us this free education, without paying a researcher to serve up the same humble pie?

Here we are with the biggest of pictures. If our clients don't see themselves, they might not see their competitors either. And that may prove no small consolation for a group looking to break-out from a listless and unassuming market. Maybe, the biggest jump on the competition is about timing: Knowing when to strike *when* the coast is clear? Put another way: Demonstrating market disinterest is the green light for rallying the release of our client's ambitions. Whether it's a campaign or a product, here's the cover we afford them:

1. They can act with impunity: What are better grounds for action than a chaotic muddle as camouflage for skirting the law?

2. They can see a world of possibility: Seeing a greater range of actions and outcomes is the basis for forming a better perspective on the *fathomable* than on the *familiar.*

3. They can prioritize: Detachment from the short-lived distractions of the moment enables clients to remain both focused on long-term goals and flexible on short-term adjustments.

So that's the value we're offering. We're showing our clients how they can put themselves in situations where favorable consequences loom larger than negative ones. That doesn't mean we know the odds. But it does mean we can foresee the impact on our clients and how those consequences should influence their decisions, their meaning, and even guiding them to see...

- What decisions are worth deciding, and

- What's better tabled because (a) the chances are remote, or (b) its beyond our reach, our sphere of influence.

Ah, the analytical luxury of pure speculation!

RESEARCH PROJECTS AS INSURANCE POLICIES

Humans react negatively to unexplained events. The tendency is so widespread that it's preferable to give a negative reason than none at all. The most popular explanation is the one that answers why sh*t happens: Why events don't play out in our favor. As Nassim Taleb likes to point out, the evocative events that we dread can cause us to *overestimate the unusual* or lie in wait for cataclysmic events:

> *"Which ... is how insurance companies thrive."* **(Taleb, 2007)**[22]

Like delusions of grandeur, these darkest wish fulfillments share a common bond with their rosier counterparts on the daydream ledger: They don't come true.

There are defining moments ingrained in our minds. The calamitous nature of a past disaster enables them to burrow deeply. They can grip the public imagination, indeed the course of history itself. Nassim talks of the *hedgehogs* that fixate on the inevitability of an unprecedented, sweeping, and odds-defying catastrophe:

> *"Falling for the narrative fallacy that makes us so blinded by one single outcome that we cannot imagine others."*

Seeing the wider playing field might intimidate some clients. Others see advantages in this great expanse of uncertainty. They look for contingencies and alternatives. They don't fixate on the precision of models and relative certainty of the known unknowns, a.k.a. probabilities.

Ray Kurzweil has said that technology is growing exponentially. And our intuition about the future is linear. To paraphrase Steve Jobs, perhaps this is why we don't expect innovation from focus groups:

> *If you asked a group of early 20th Century consumers what kinds of transport will make their lives more traveled and their schedules busier, they might suggest faster horses. No one would have clamored for horseless carriages before any roads were paved. But that didn't kill the car in its cradle – only the forecast for fast horses.*

To riff on Nassim Taleb, (who's borrowing from Warren Buffet)...

- Don't ask the barber if you need a haircut

- Don't ask an academic if what he does is relevant

- Don't rail against political ads and then donate money to politicians

Self-interest is frowned on in public. It is pervasive in private. Hence, the strong association of the Knowledge-ABLED prevails between harboring suspicions and confirming them through unauthorized access or *overheard remarks*.

<u>**Presentation Voice**</u>

The first rule of presentation etiquette is the use of the first party voice by the presenter.

The *Informal We* is a casual way to infer a shared understanding or priority. It's an understated way for bringing clients into tacit agreement:

> *We have a common history and a mutual aim to this project. Therefore, 'we' respond similarly to the evidence presented and conclusions drawn.*

However, it's positively toxic to those questioning their membership in this agreement circle. The Informal We backfires when the speaker presumes a false unity, an overreach of who we're speaking for.

The *Royal We* is a rhetorical device that moms used on their kids to school them in the etiquette of the social courtesies and graces upheld by the family name. This possessive flourish comes across as stuffy and elitist to our presentees if we...

- Act like know-it-alls,
- Can substitute our experience for everyone else's, and
- Are too proud to endure opinions that conflict with our own.

The Informal We is not self-important. It does not presume to be the final word. It's an opening for an informed discussion about the state of the market, or the pulse of a community. It's keeping careful watch on the players and connecting the dots as a trend-watcher. That's when the 'Informal We' is the way to go for presenting a base of facts that confers both openness and authority.

What about when the Knowledge-ABLED are not only the presenters but presenting original research? We are the source of the trends that we present on our blogs and to would-be customers. We're also the authors behind the numbers. Are we buttoned down and inscrutable? Mad scientists? A dash of the *Royal We* here benefits us as presenters in three ways:

1. Presenters are perceived as doers.[23]

2. It scales the size of our operations in the minds of our audience to a larger, more established firm.

3. We're seen as delegators, conferring authority, stature.

<u>**Personality Types**</u>

Over the course of this book, we have witnessed many dichotomies. We've considered opposable forces or diametrical conditions, representing different ends of a spectrum of outcomes. We think of the continuums of credibility and authenticity, or the fork in the road between the fact and opinion-based questions we first encountered in **Unit One**.

The left and right brain forms another powerful dialectic. As presenters, we need to engage both modes of thinking as complementary to our problem solving. Here's how those forces play out in terms of evidence-gathering:

FIGURE 5.20: Left and Right Brain Evidence-gathering

Left brain	Right brain
Rational	imaginative
Linear	perceptual (metaphorical)
Logical	intuitive, whimsical
Sequential	visual (pictures, gestures)
Literal	ambiguous, paradoxical
Objective	subjective
time-sensitive	time-free
Accurate	Approximate

An important takeaway for researcher-presenters is not to favor one approach over the other. Instead we encourage both sides to remain on speaking terms: Supporting one another for testing rationales and weighing outcomes.

The key is knowing when we're favoring one side at the expense of the other. For instance, shortchanging a multitude of viewpoints because of a dominant view demonstrates a lack of curiosity and a face value acceptance of the status quo. That's a left brain approach to a right brain exercise. In contrast, an unquestioning acceptance of one's direct experience is no substitute for well-established laws, measurements, and patterns governing the physical world.

The trick is understanding where to strike the balance between longstanding precedent and the specific circumstances where we need to apply our sense-making.

From Homework to Billable Work

Do we enlist the hard left and the soft right of our brain matter in our problem-solving? Either way, our presentation chops are best served by going the distance, and then some. That means proving our mettle by playing out alternate scenarios. This is different than taking in conflicting arguments, or clashing views. This is investing in several plausible outcomes, with no allegiances to any specific agendas, or priorities of the people involved.

One way to address this is to revisit our old crony, mister risk. This means talking through the uncertainties that our clients must confront.Those are concerns where the rosy forecasts and the fundraising goals fall short. Presenting a glass half-full and half-empty scenario is critical for connecting the research we've done to the results we're trying to help our customers achieve.

Playing out best and worst case scenarios not only proves that we know our stuff. We're also pragmatists who can adjust our services to fit fast-moving and complex situations. Scripting these two different outcomes also shows that we don't just want *in*, but are willing to put ourselves on the line for clients.

For instance, we might share the risk by reducing our upfront fee with the agreement of a greater upside, should the client's program meet or exceed its goals. This shows that we not only have skin the game, but stand behind a performance-based commitment.

It's all Black and White (and partly gray)

Now let's go from the abstraction of brain cells to the bare details of our case. There are many factors involved with any investigation. At the outset, let's consider what we know for sure and where the speculation ensues. That's when conclusions start to form and our work begins: How we substantiate our own conclusions about the case. Here's where those less-than-foregone conclusions coalesce around those inexhaustible details:

FIGURE 5.21: The Continuum of Uncertainty

Certainty	Uncertainty
Names and dates	Interpretations
Crime scene evidence	Perceptions
Personal records	Motivations & influences
Past deeds	Personal values and judgments
Rules and laws	Personal reward and justice system

REASONABLE CERTAINTY AND HONEST DOUBTS

As any veteran will tell you, a case brimming over with detail does nothing to guarantee that the evidence is mounting in favor of a specific outcome or conclusion. At a certain point, we need to take a hard right turn from the left brain exhibits of crime scenes and ballistics analysis to the right brain of probable motives and pay-outs. That means a most decidedly *third person* perspective on our *first person* search targets.

For example, one of the best pathways into the intentions of case-relevant suspects is to examine their frame of reference. This means looking at the personal networks and extended communities of those under investigation. Judging a suspect's ultimate intention straddles the line of *knowing the unknowable.*

Looking more broadly at our target's frame of reference is a useful, if not foolproof way to understand their influences, and reward system for carrying out potentially criminal actions.

FIGURE 5.22: The Continuum of Reasonable Certainty and Honest Doubt

Reasonable Certainty	*Honest Doubt*
Community Awareness	Self-Justification
Common Knowledge	Self-Deception
Advice and Guidance	Intuition
Safe Harbor	Self-Image
Community Interest	Self-Discipline

SECTION 5:4 | Project Presentation –

The Presentation as Exhibit

So we've arrived at game day ... the unveiling ... the truth-letting

The sudden death overtime round where we show our cards in arrangements made to help our clients play their own hands, whether the stakes are around...

- Weathering a crisis,

- Gaining first mover advantage, or

- Sizing up the probable motives of a person of interest in a murder plot.

There are three irreducible factors from which all final presentations are judged: (1) The client's prior pre-existing knowledge, (2) new awareness we provide, and (3) investment in the outcomes we recommend. These success factors are tempered by our own...

- **Obstruction:** We're not being told the whole story – at least how our clients understand it.

- **Transparency:** Our clients hold a layperson's view from outsourcing their research process to Google.

Marking the distance we traveled between an unaided Google search and the value we're providing, is one roadmap worth pulling out *before* we share our findings. In fact, it's every bit as important as retracing our first tentative footsteps, from before we familiarized ourselves with our search targets, topics in play, and details pertinent to our cases.

We would be doing our clients and ourselves a disservice if we don't capture the original inferences that fall into our laps. The comparison is this: Simple keyword searches processed through complex algorithms, versus the value provided by the tools and frameworks we apply as Knowledge-ABLED investigators.

MARKING THE DISTANCE

One of the best ways to guide the client through our investigative process is to track our progress through the SPM sequences we established back in **Unit One**. A well-documented SPM form will include (1) the unfolding of our query formations, (2) tool selection, (3) source inventory, and (4) key indicators such as a list of pointers and/or project corrections prompted by our failsafes.

How do we evidence this? We can showcase the value of our services by demonstrating how we use query formation to cut through the generalities to the most salient, accurate, and ultimately useful findings. For example...

- Assessing the uniqueness of the target (how easy is it to google the person?) and commonality of search terms

- Judging the difference between what individuals or organizations say about themselves, versus what others say about them, e.g., credibility testing

- Comparing the priorities and references used by clients with the popular associations cited by other stakeholders, including rivals, customers, and other channels of opinion

The next step is to show how the background research extends into the foreground. That means how our digital investigations prompt us to seek out, and conduct primary interviews and fact-finding:

1. What were the interview questions we drafted?

2. How were they based on our background checks?

3. Where do those interviews fill in the loose-ends and conjecture from our search logs?

INTEGRATING THE PIECES, PACKAGING YOUR PRESENTATION

Research is often just one aspect of an investigation. In some cases, it is the sole reason behind a client's request. In both cases typical reports often contain specific sections.

1. Statement of Investigation Objective

The baseline that sets that roadmap in motion is a restatement of the project aims as well as any revised or adjusted scopes of the work. This is a contractual pledge to the client. It's also a binding commitment by the consulting researcher to maintain professional standards. The researcher will work within established ethical guidelines while understanding that...

- No protocol or set of responsibilities can directly address all actions, outcomes, and issues that are brought to bear in the conducting of any given investigation.

- The researcher will endeavor to avoid relationships or circumstances that would jeopardize her independence or rigor of the methods used to capture, disseminate, and analyze the findings contained in her report. **(Mitchell, 2011)**[24]

2. Information Supplied by the Client

Another table-setter is the opportunity to restate the significant client discussions and conferrals after the original premise for the project was reached. This is an essential reckoning of a fixed objective with the fluid and dynamic nature of independent investigations. Two additional dynamics are at play here:

1. Being *listened to* is a big deal. Seeing our requirements and consultations in writing is an important reminder of agreements made prior to the project.

2. It's also a reminder to the client which aspects of their prior knowledge they decide to share on background with the project team.

3. Methodology Section

This is the least requested and most often referred to section on projects that involve client larger groups, often with competing agendas and uneven participation. The methodology section does not change. It helps inform or reacquaint team members with the approaches used to secure the findings presented. In the Methodology section, it helps to explain to show how we'll arrive at conclusions before we draw them by...

- Referencing the tools and frameworks we've applied as Knowledge-ENABLED investigators to maintain our independence.
- Doing this without sacrificing diligence, or succumbing to the self-selecting nature of personal biases, i.e. the need to be right.
- Sequencing the repeatable steps used to test assumptions and assimilate new findings.

4. Findings

The results we choose to include in our discussions or slides should be actionable or supportive of our conclusions and recommendations. There's always room to append the raw data, and unabridged evidence in a separate file. In the Findings section there are various perspectives from which we can address our presentations. These include:

1. Quantification (counts specific to search targets based on the source selection and time frame comparisons we saw in a survey model like **The Biggest Picture** in Section 5.1)

2. Project tracking (event-specific alerts and source-specific notifications)

3. Precedents and baselines (comparing this investigation to similar probes based on norms and expectations)

5. Conclusions

There's always a temptation to over-explain the validation process: Why we come down on one side or another. The explanatory power evidence of *conclusive evidence* releases the intoxicant we call *near-certainty*. Never underestimate the value of reducing uncertainty – even when those reductions may not be where the client is pinning their hopes. The Conclusion section states your confidence level based on what the search results tell you about the case you're conducting:

1. When you are uncertain, your confidence level is *hypothetical*.

2. When you are sure, your confidence level is *conclusive*.

6. Recommendations

A good consultant proves their mettle by attempting to put themselves out of business at the project close. Most clients (paying ones anyway) have their attention on our presentations. They also keep one eye on any scope creep required to nail down the loose-ends we can't resolve in this phase. That's why the recommendations section should resist any attempt to speculate beyond the evidence contained in the report at-hand.

There needs to be *enough to go on* even if we're suggesting an expansion of the existing effort. If not, a delay of the meeting date may be the best revised scheduling.

7. Repeatability

It's the omission of showing the panel, the client, the board, city elders or whoever has enough skin in this game to realize it's not just us. It's not just the case we're making. It's that anyone else without a vested interest in the outcome could reach the same conclusion.

The web is especially persuasive if we can prove that we're not gaming systems, or tipping our hands. We're simply assembling what any bystander with our research skills could figure out, without the lawyers and the news reporters. The flip side is that we need to make this as plain and obvious to our audience as it may have been difficult and even painstaking to produce.

Did I mention that can sometimes be a challenge?

<u>Getting Input from Collaborators</u>

Up until now, the journey of the Knowledge-ABLED has all the trappings of a solo mission. Even when we introduce the more social elements of our investigations, we are striking a largely independent chord in our singular pursuit of unvarnished evidence. Searching by nature is an introverted pastime. Searching out loud is the way we question search engines. That said, conversations between researchers and the databases they converse with are largely solitary, telepathic affairs. At least until they see the light of day in the presentation of their findings.

The lone researcher slaving away at an unblinking screen is a plausible scenario for most the work we've done together in **Units Two** and **Three**. That convention goes out to the window once our BS sniffers are pressed against the window of our presentations. That window is not restricted to the clients who've retained us. In fact, the more solo our journey, the more incentive we have to open that window to colleagues and associates. Who specifically are sound candidates for this collaboration?

Ideally, they have a domain expertise that's relevant to the (1) topics, (2) locations, (3) policies, and/or (4) client objectives you've been retained to investigate, or even support. But that association could backfire if the connection extends to the actual case, social networks, and communities impacted by the findings. Professional interest and personal detachment will ensure the trust required to build on the feedback and suggestions one anticipates in pre-presentation mode.

PLANNING THE PRESENTATION

Verbalizing our patter is quite a different calculation from tabular graphics, and color palettes. However, it's the single biggest non-editorial presentation decision we'll make. Do we fly solo through the final ascent? Would a co-pilot or at least a co-presenter reinforce the degree of diligence and care we've exerted for the duration? The camaraderie alone may prove a welcome respite from the relentless pursuit of a disciplined, but often isolating discovery process.

If so, has our co-presenter bought into our findings? Can they add their own convictions to the resonating strength of our recommendations?

It helps to do a hand-off, not just in terms of voices, but in stepping through a workflow process. The most compelling presentations give the audience a sense of the interplay. This is the back-and-forth that happens between a stakeholder with an issue or a question, and a subject expert with an answer or an approach. Hearing different voices also keeps sessions varied and interesting. Pad your presentation with invitations for responding. Structure interaction time into each section.

What about our own presentation style? Body language aside, there are some generic flourishes that cut across most presentation deliveries. Whether we're teaming up or soloing, we'll need to modulate our voice, and maintain eye contact across the room (especially with those distracted by texts and smart phone prattle). Avoid the temptation to read the bullets verbatim off presentation slides, use some well-executed hand gestures to underscore points. Take extra care to smooth the sectional transitions, with responses or without.

<u>Logistics</u>

There's the additional dynamic of the room we'll be working in addition to our voicing:

- ■ **Room Setting** – Can you select the room set up to meet the interactivity needs of your presentation? It's a long shot we'll have a say in room size, acoustics, seating arrangements, and white, unwelcome noise, e.g. the droning of the overactive air conditioning units.

- **Group Size** – How many and who will be in the audience? Audience size determines the level of interactivity. Typically any room with 25 attendees or greater requires that the Q&A be delayed until the end of your talk. For smaller groups, it may be advisable to capture feedback in real-time on a flip chart. Then re-engage those questions and comments on the back-end of the discussion. For larger groups, repeat questions before answering them. Viola! All participants hear the same question. Repeating it buys you time to compose your answer.

- **Prior History** – How well will the audience know the topic? For example, will there be various levels of knowledge: Beginner, intermediate, advanced? Can we draw the audience out with a polling topic to involve them? Eyeballing the number of hands raised helps us to figure out awareness levels and exposes the audience to the same real-time responses.

- **Texting Questions** – For the larger audiences, invite Q&A in advance. In public settings, text questions to a pre-selected phone number or Twitter feed. This spares the clumsy orchestration of having audience members step to a microphone to fire off an off-color or politically-loaded question.

- **Oprah Moves** – Be mindful about leaving the podium if you are serving on a panel. We don't wish to show-up our fellow presenters. On the other hand, if *we have the floor*, then working the room may be an appropriate way to capture the audience, and keep them engaged.

THE ABILITY TO INFLUENCE

So those are the building blocks of presenting our research. One aspect not typically addressed in the elements of effective presentation styles are the outcomes we're trying to reach. Think of it a Dale Carnegie advice bible on *how to win arguments and influence people.*

It's not just enough to access data. It's not just about having a seat at the table. It's not even enough if you have the authority to ask the tough, direct questions to commanding figures. Those are the luminaries that are squirming in their witness chairs, hoping you won't ask them. What does help is eye contact. What helps is when your eyes are persuaded by your own words. Remember, your eyes have the capacity to talk, along with your voice *as* you're presenting.

Launching a web investigation implies the use of tools and resources that anyone could use at that same witness table or from a WIFI-enabled cave around the globe. That common virtual touch is both the greatest challenge for virtual investigators and our greatest opportunity. With that said, here are those trade-offs. How to overcome the obstacles and ride the advantages, without missing a beat:

1) Stand up to Information Overload

There is a direct connection between too much information and too little forethought. Mainly, it's what to do when the overload hits. Anxiety has a way of ruling out options. That stress is magnified when we feel like an answer or a resolution is at-hand. It's just buried under a blizzard of databases and websites.

Rather than step back and regroup, it's often tempting to retreat into the very habits that caused us to freak-out in the first place. One of these havens is not so much a habit as a fantasy. It's the temptation of succumbing to the information myths that cloud our thinking, and pressure us into the poor choices we make when we're *used* by information.

Remember, being Knowledge-ABLED is both a defense against information glut, and a rally cry. It means we're an ally to our collaborators, clients, and communities in the quest to take informed action within a clarifying set of foreseeable outcomes.

2) Defy the Oversimplification of the World According to Google

One of the all-time leading urban legends is the notion that Google and the web are interchangeable. Need a free piece of information? Give Google a few hints about the person and their whereabouts, and Google will breathlessly deliver their every mention.

What does hold some water is the notion that until something better comes along, Google is the de facto radar for establishing what a casual search can yield in the way of public knowledge about everyday people – particularly those with uncommon first names and surnames.

3) Don't Overreact

One common and counterproductive information strategy is the tendency to over-communicate. This tendency is inspired by the false assumption: For every incoming message, there is an outgoing response.

Think we owe it to every tree that ever fell in any forest to read all our correspondence? We can't let it manage us if the ultimate goal is to stay on top of our workload. It's not as if the world is waiting on our immediate response. No one is going to need an ambulance if we don't answer straight away. Separate the urgency of the matter, from the desperation of the person provoking us.

If that's easier in theory than practice, consider this escape hatch: One liberating aspect of RSS readers is that we can let hundreds, even thousands of posts pile up without the fear that we're flushing down some unrecoverable treasure. Another great thing about RSS feeds is that we can search the granular details without needing to read, scan, or even browse through pages of search results. Web pages bearing no resemblance to our priorities or even passing interests.

Information needs to make time for us.

4) Getting a Grip on Attention Surplus Disorder

This made-up malady is the common impulse of triggering a refresh on your favorite communications tools to steal attention away from the task-at-hand. You need to disconnect from the web if you need to focus on presenting your thoughts in an original way. Presenting arguments, supporting claims, and analyzing reams of evidence means one thing for certain: Synthesizing many ideas and inputs. Many of us can't do this through screens for the single reason that the temptation is too great to dodge headlong into ... more inputs!

It is necessary to transition from the collection to the analytical phase of your research so that you can process, interpret, and prioritize the information you've synthesized into that range of clarifying options. Those next recommended steps that underpin your own unexpected findings, measured conclusions, and plausible outcomes.

Approaching this transition with a sense of closure and completeness is what we mean by *logging off* with confidence. So remember – you *do* have to clear your head – maybe even turn off your iPhone, and go for a stroll.

5) Dealing with Continuous Partial Attention

Another affliction on the receiving end of attention surplus is "continuous partial attention." That's what happens when your audience is tapping its collective fingers on the cracked knuckles of their smart phone keys.

We're talking about an impairment that runs deeper than the most uncooperative witness, or the most elusive search term. That's the inability of your audience to stay with you through an extended discussion, complex argument, or drawn-out sequence of events and speculations. At the same time, the group you're addressing is not being rude on purpose.

They are not tuning out. They may even be keeping up with you (and other pressing concerns simultaneously). Continuous partial attention is that clashing combination of connectedness and distraction. The key to combating it? Finding the correct mental file drawer where our audience puts information they will access *after* the presentation.

6) Failure is an Option

"Fragmented stories of partial failure create more learning than formal documents summarizing best practice."

– David Snowden

Fear of failure is a great galvanizing tool. Unnecessary risks and avoidable blunders are two surefire ways to sharpen the listening capacity of our audience members. On the subject of failure, let's own up to ours. Let's avoid terms like *success* and *wins,* and all things triumphant.

That doesn't mean we have to talk down our accomplishments or use false modesty when we deliver great value. It means that failure is not only an option. It's a requirement. Mistakes are not just something to own up to. They are worth taking credit for. Learning happens by design – not accident. Mistakes are neutral. Learn from them and they're highly instructive. Repeat them and we deserve to lose our presenter license. The worst repeatable error is that the same person makes the same mistake time and time again. The second worst error is to pay for the same learning over and over.

7) Seeking out Apparent Conflicts of Interest

The greatest contradiction between people and how they use information is conflict-of-interest. The notion that what they say in public runs contrary to what they do in private. Hypocrisy is often associated with the variance between how people behave as figureheads in their professional roles, and as individuals in their personal lives. Often this means taking their lofty titles and leadership roles to speak for the group they represent, when their private dealings advance their own interests ahead of the organizations they represent.

Not all hypocrisies are deliberately self-serving. Sometimes they are based on self-deception. Sometimes these escapes are willful flights of fantasy. As we saw in **Unit One**, we're oblivious to our own blindspots. Sometimes we invent our own histories, not because we're deluding ourselves, but because we're all too aware of the social demands of the workplace.

For example, our resumes are self-constructed upwardly-advancing career projections based on merit and well-deserved promotions. Such fabrications often cover over our flaws, skill gaps, unceremonious firings, or other disconnects that cast doubt and confusion on the image we're projecting as potential hires. Other common social rituals like the filing of tax returns are another way that we present a selective fact base to an official authority, as a way of offsetting another societal obligation.

8) We're all Subjective Experts

While appearing well-accomplished to one audience, we show our destitute side to the government. Is it a conflict of interest to pay lower taxes? How plausibly can we plead poverty to the tax collector? These are subjective questions, dependent on who you ask. Behaviors that govern conflict-of-interest are a more reliable bellwether. They have as much to do with the audience, as the actors for whom they sit in judgment.

Put another way, most of us *fudge* a little on our tax returns. The more productive result in your conflict-of-interest investigation comes when you ask how the institution handles this common practice. When does one person's fudging land themselves at the top of the suspected cheaters pile? When do the actions of an individual taxpayer trigger counter-actions – an IRS audit for example? Conducting conflict-of-interest investigations are not limited to retrieving the public, legal, and financial records of one individual. If that were so, anyone with a credit card and a open browser window could meet the challenge. A Knowledge-ABLED investigator anticipates the actions an authority may take based on the way it handles the case in question.

9) Gathering an Influential Perspective

This kind of analysis is not limited to brushes with the law and the work of enforcement agencies. Sometimes the potential range of outcomes is not about serving jail time. Maybe it's not punitive at all:

> 1. Perhaps you're estimating the kind of professional fees you command as a subject matter expert?
>
> 2. You're in the running for a job whose funding depends on sources outside of the hiring organization?
>
> 3. Maybe you need to weigh treatment options for a loved one, afflicted unexpectedly with a serious illness?

Regardless of the particulars, our investigation skills will help determine an outcome for our clients and ourselves based on: (1) The outcomes our sponsors can expect, and (2) our own negotiating position with the groups and institutions we are trying to influence.

This is not a *me or you* proposition. This is a how-do-I-fit-into-the-broader-scope-of-what-can-happen-given-past-history orientation. Ultimately we all want the higher-paying position. We want the cure to heal our loved ones. But these aspirations are not ranked highest, or even buried in search results. Your influence will be felt when you can speak with authority about the greater concerns and priorities on the minds of the hiring managers, funding sources, and clinical trial sponsors: In short, the decision-makers who would weigh in your favor.

And regardless of what *that* message is, your outsider status makes you the ideal messenger.

10) Don't Let Google Over-complicate Your Own World

As we saw in Section 1.4: Becoming Knowledge-ABLED, the standard version of Google departed from the reality stage in 2012. This rendered all search results as subjective. No two user sessions were certain to produce the same outcomes. Ever since, virtual investigators have been left to ponder:

1. How can we be offering transparency when an algorithm is intercepting our searches?

2. How can we promise repeatability when our click patterns and profile data skew our results away from those of our presentation audience?

The answer is that a promising number of search engine alternatives have cropped up. They not only refrain from tracking us, but enable the same queries to produce the same outcomes, regardless of who's formulations they are. Duck Duck Go, Wolfram Alpha, MetaGer, and Disconnect Search all deliver the benefits of search syntax, semantics, and operators without the need to sacrifice granularity, or surrender personal data. Best of all, you can turn the URLs generated by your queries over to your clients (the way search logs were intended). Scooch over to the passenger seat, and watch their personal investment in the project soar.

FIGURE 5.23: Elements of Presentation Style

Element	Presentation Goal
Audience	The Statement of the Investigation Objective will rehash the explicit goals of the assigned research. The remainder of the report is governed by an implicit goal – anticipating the reader's needs.
Tone	Research is delivered even-tempered and even-handedly. The researcher is dispassionate, reserved, never shrill, and resists the temptation to exaggerate, editorialize, or accept unsupported evidence.
Movement	Like our own learning curves, a decent presentation progresses from initial impressions to tested assumptions. It's not static and doesn't restate idle facts. There is a sense of order without contrivances or forced narratives.
Format	A winning presentation looks smart on the page. That means being easy to absorb, skim quickly, and extract salient information. It refrains from unrelenting text and includes tables and graphics to summarize findings, generalize patterns, and support conclusions.
Investment	How much time will they spend reading our document once we're done presenting? Consider this when deciding how much detail to communicate through supporting charts and addendums.

The Experiential Side of Presenting

It's not an accident than SPM reflects the cardinal rule of reporting: The journalism convention for constructing a news article, covering the *who, what, when, where, why,* and *how* of the events we're chronicling. While the sequence has been reordered, the retelling of our research can be conveyed through our discovery process: Where we are, and how we got there, follow the same script. That makes it easier to share our discoveries and the spirit of discovery in our presentations.

Think of it as comparing notes rather than favoring one competing version of events and their significance. That means capturing first impressions as a basis for involving the client in our collective research experience. It's also a compelling reminder for how off we may have been on our original hunches.

Naturally, it helps to humanize the data side when we're summarizing the stories that numbers can tell. But behind every persuasive analyst is a healthy, lucid comparison, relating tables and charts to the people and anecdotes they address.

FIGURE 5.24: Journalism 101: Unpacking News Reports through the Inverted Pyramid[25]

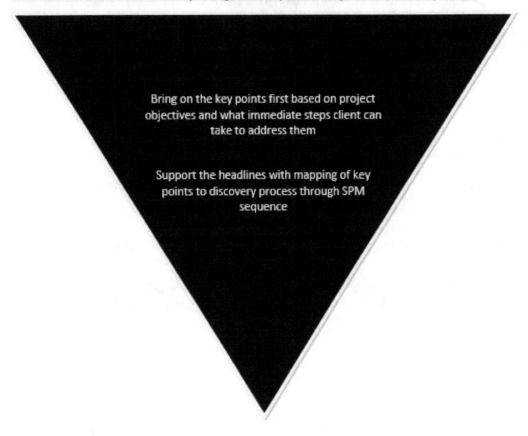

Bring on the key points first based on project objectives and what immediate steps client can take to address them

Support the headlines with mapping of key points to discovery process through SPM sequence

UNIT FIVE: WRAPPING

FOCUSING ON PRESENTATION

Unit Five tied together the collection, filtering, and evaluation methods introduced and modeled in the first four units. Those practices were surfaced in a survey or quantitative approach to capturing search-based outcomes ('The Biggest Picture'). We then looked at the social currency of our research findings through the information bartering opportunities afforded by blogging communities and domain experts. In Section 5.3 we examined some intentional ways to involve our social circles in the packaging of our research. We finished the unit with the mechanics of delivering these reports to our clients and communities.

In **Unit Six**, the book's curriculum will conclude with a Knowledge-ABLED use case based on the professional transformation of a commercial video producer to an educational media consultant. This use case guides us through the false starts and initial frustrations to the firmer footing and ultimate confidence-building that comes with being Knowledge-ENABLED.

All relevant practices, frameworks, and search strategies in the case study are referenced to the specific units and chapters where they're introduced and demonstrated. For instance, our use case subject entrepreneur plots out his research goals and supporting tasks through the **Search Project Management** model.

Our protagonist applies the principles of **Site Selection** and **Oceans, Lakes, and Ponds** to determine his sources, generate business leads, and build his understanding of the market and its growth potential. Finally, our practitioner uses the **Provider Conjugation Framework** as a way of engaging the very same business contacts that first landed on his radar as search targets.

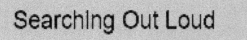

[1] Robert I. Sutton, "How to Be a Good Boss in a Bad Economy," Harvard Business Review, June, 2009

[2] Eli Pariser, "The Bubble Filter," TED Conference, February 2011

[3] Kenneth M. Bilby, "The General: David Sarnoff and the Rise of the Communications Industry." New York: Harper & Row, 1986

[4] Andrew Morris-Friedman, "Hindsight of the Future," Hampshire College, 1984

[5] This was a reliable audience size for viewing the Academy Awards prior to the arrival of social media.

[6] Onpoint Radio, "iPad & The Daily, AOL-HuffPo: Reading The Media-News Future," February 7, 2011

[7] Mickey Meese, "Who's the Boss, You or Your Gadget?" New York Times, February 5, 2011

[8] Feed Demon has a notable presence in Unit Six's Knowledge-ABLED Case Study.

[9] Google Insights for Search was discontinued in 2012.

[10] Vicki Abelson, "Divorce Internet Style," Huffington Post, December 28, 2011

[11] Robert Pozen, NPR, OnPoint, "The Economy in 2012 and Your Money," January 3, 2012

[12] Darlene Adams, "Romantic Deception: The Six Signs He's Lying," Dr. Sally Caldwell and Darlene E. Adams, CreateSpace, 2010

[13] Assuming we acknowledge the line between civil liberties and hate speech.

[14] However, it's no accident that RSS is ineffectual for tracking news feed activities on social

media. Such monitoring would pose a commercial challenge to social media platforms.

[15] To restrict all information providers to Bay State-based publishers.

[16] The forward slash and asterisk indicates that all indexed pages are included under each site root.

[17] Ibid, Morville

[18] Nassim Nicholas Taleb, "The Black Swan," Random House, 2007

[19] James O'Toole, Warren Bennis, "Culture of Candor," Harvard Business Review, June, 2009

[20] "Fast and Slow: Pondering The Speed Of Thought," NPR, October 27, 2011

[21] Ibid, Taleb

[22] Ibid, Taleb

[23] This stands in contrast to us thinker-researchers, crunching the numbers in the back office.

[24] Bill Mitchell, "Ethics Guidelines for Poynter Publishing," March 3, 2011, http://www.poynter.org/archived/about-poynter/20209/ethics-guidelines-for-poynter-publishing

[25] Note that we considered another pyramid inversion in **Unit Three**: Figure 3.45: The Pyramid of 20th Century Institutional (Source) Credibility. This infographic correlates the stature of traditional media sources with their circulation numbers.

About the Author

Marc Solomon has been a knowledge architect, search manager, and competitive intelligence director in the acronym-laced world of strategic consulting (PwC, PRTM, FSG, and FIND/SVP) as well as tech services (BellSouth, Avid Technology, and Hyperion Solutions).

He currently works in the office of the CTO at The Hartford insurance company. He's presented on search, metadata, taxonomy, and Knowledge-ABLED practices through the Boston KM Forum, Enterprise Search Summit, Gilbane, and SIKM (Systems Integrators KM Leaders).

From 2005 to 2010 he was an adjunct professor in Boston University's Professional Investigation Program where he trained budding PIs on using the web to crack criminal cases, including instruction in digital media research and information literacy.

Mr. Solomon is a contributing columnist to several trade magazines on enterprise knowledge tools, practices and business cases including Searcher, Baseline, and KM World where he contributed a year-long "reality series" of SharePoint case deployment profiles. Solomon has addressed the realities of day-to-day content management as an expert blogger in the AIIM SharePoint Community. As a search expert and knowledge guru, he has decades of experience in teaching students how to become more information literate.

Most recently he launched an Open Source Intelligence (OSINT) program at the Montague Book Mill for mid-career professionals as founder of the Society for Useful Information, whose mission is to improve the quality of digital literacy and research practices throughout Western New England.

Solomon holds a BA in the History of Technology from Hampshire College and a Masters in Professional Studies from the Graduate School of Political Management at George Washington University. He lives with his wife Patty, Jaspurr the cat, and occasionally their three grown children in a home with no smart speakers and where no one searches in silence.

www.ingramcontent.com/pod-product-compliance
Lightning Source LLC
Chambersburg PA
CBHW060154060326
40690CB00018B/4107